Overcoming Compulsive Washing

FREE
YOUR MIND
FROM
OCD

Paul R. Munford, Ph.D.

New Harbinger Publications, Inc.

Copyright © 2005 by Paul R. Munford
New Harbinger Publications, Inc.
5674 Shattuck Avenue
Oakland, CA 94609

Cover design by Amy Shoup
Acquired by Tesilya Hanauer
Edited by Spencer Smith
Text design by Tracy Marie Carlson

ISBN 1-57224-405-4 Paperback
Library of Congress Cataloging in Publication Data on file

Distributed in Canada by Raincoast Books
All Rights Reserved
Printed in the United States of America

New Harbinger Publications' Web site address: www.newharbinger.com

Library of Congress Cataloging-in-Publication Data

Munford, Paul R.
  Overcoming compulsive washing : free your mind from OCD / Paul R. Munford.
    p. cm.
  Includes bibliographical references.
  ISBN 1-57224-405-4
  1. Obsessive-compulsive disorder—Popular works. 2. Compulsive washing—Popular works.
I. Title.
  RC533.M86 2005
  616.85'227—dc22
                                     2005010588

07   06   05
10   9   8   7   6   5   4   3   2   1
First printing

With Love
to
Alison and Chris

Contents

Introduction   1

Chapter 1
What You Need to Know to Help Yourself   5

Chapter 2
Contamination Fears and Other Triggers   27

Chapter 3
Self-Assessment   51

Chapter 4
Face, Embrace, and Erase the Fear   71

Chapter 5
Exposure Exercises for Fear of Anxiety and Illness   91

Chapter 6
Exposure Exercises for Fear of Urine and Feces   113

Chapter 7
Exposure Exercises for Fear of Blood   129

Chapter 8
Hindrances, Helpers, and Holding On to Success   143

Resources   155

References   159

Introduction

This book is for people with obsessive-compulsive disorder (OCD) who have washing compulsions, one of the most common subtypes of the disorder. People with this subtype of OCD are obsessed by irrational thoughts and images of becoming contaminated by germs, dirt, radiation, chemicals, environmental contaminants, and the like. They fear that contamination could lead to illness or life-threatening diseases, or to high anxiety and even nervous breakdowns. To protect themselves from these consequences, they attempt to avoid, as completely as possible, situations perceived as contaminated. But this is impossible, and when contact with contaminants occurs they resort to compulsive washing to offset anxiety and prevent disastrous health consequences. These behaviors bring relief and some small feeling of safety that is temporary, lasting only until the next bout with contamination. Doing any number of ordinary, everyday activities poses the risk of slip-ups for everyone, and we usually take reasonable measures to prevent them. But for the person with OCD of the washing type, reasonable measures become monstrous burdens. They wash and rewash in hopes of preventing disasters, and find, paradoxically, that the more they wash, the more they must continue to wash.

Furthermore, the security they are seeking remains out of reach, and as the washing intensifies they can feel hopelessly trapped in endless cycles of washing rituals. This book is designed to help people overcome their washing rituals and be free from their irrational fears of contamination, unending anxiety, and illness. On achieving this goal, they will feel relief and the freedom to go about the world with a joy of life that comes from casting off a burden, which many have endured for years.

This book is not a substitute for professional help. It is for people with mild to moderate OCD who wish to try a self-directed approach. If you're seeing a mental-health professional who doesn't specialize in treating OCD, this book can be used by both of you to treat your OCD. Many people are reluctant to seek help for various reasons. One of the most frequent is fear of the unknown. If you are one of these people, or know someone who is, this book can provide information that might lessen your fears and encourage you to get treatment.

The book can also be helpful to mental-health professionals who wish to learn more about behavior therapy approaches to OCD. It can be used to treat a person with mild to moderate washing compulsions, in conjunction with consultation from an OCD expert.

The stories herein are all true-life examples of OCD sufferers. Their names and personal information have been changed to keep their identities confidential.

THIS BOOK IS A TREATMENT TOOL

This book will show you how to carry out the same behavior therapy techniques that I use when treating patients in my office. These methods have been scientifically proven to be effective for eliminating obsessions and compulsions. They involve various forms of exposure therapy. This is a method wherein the person learns how to desensitize themselves to obsessional fears that trigger compulsions. The therapist functions as a teacher, coach, or consultant. That is, the therapist teaches you how to do behavioral exercises that can bring about the elimination of the irrational fears that drive washing rituals. As it is with most learning activities, practice is required. Specifically, you will need to devote one to two hours per day to the behavioral exercises over a period of four to six weeks, depending on the severity of your disorder. Of course, the more work you do, the faster you'll receive the benefits from it.

SCOPE OF THE BOOK

The book provides general information on OCD, how it works, and how it is treated. It explains the scientific basis for, and the use of, behavior therapy for eliminating or reducing symptoms. You'll then be given step-by-step instructions for developing and practicing a series of exercises that will neutralize your fears and thereby eliminate the need for compulsive washing. The exercises target washing rituals triggered by fear of harm to your emotional or physical health as a result of contamination from toxins. The book concludes with recommendations for maintaining your treatment gains and information for significant others about ways they can help or hinder your recovery.

ABOUT THE AUTHOR

I'm a clinical psychologist who has been practicing for over thirty years. In the mid-1970s, I was introduced to my first case of OCD. It involved a seven-year-old youngster who had fears of contamination from dirt and germs. At that time, the disorder was considered to be rare. Now we know that it is fairly prevalent. Back then, it was considered not responsive to treatment. Now we know that it is quite treatable. I had success with the youngster by using treatment techniques based on the research of Edna Foa, who is internationally recognized as a leading authority on the disorder. This experience of seeing the youngster and his mother relieved of suffering by the use of behavior therapy was inspiring, the feeling of which is rekindled by working with people who have OCD.

I continued working with OCD patients and eventually developed and directed the behavior therapy component of the OCD Partial Hospitalization Program at the Neuropsychiatric Institute, UCLA, which was the first of its type in the nation. After retiring from the university as an adjunct professor of psychiatry, I relocated to the Sacramento area where I teach cognitive behavioral therapy as a clinical professor at the Department of Psychiatry, University of California, Davis School of Medicine. Missing my involvement with patients with OCD at UCLA, I developed and direct an intensive day treatment program for OCD sufferers here in Sacramento.

CHAPTER I

What You Need to Know to Help Yourself

Until recently, obsessive-compulsive disorder (OCD) was considered rare. Now we know that millions have the problem, and there are two scientifically proven treatments for it—behavior therapy and medications. Though OCD can be a devastating disorder, treatment can enable 75 percent of sufferers to significantly reduce or eliminate their symptoms.

On the surface, OCD appears to be senseless, capricious, unpredictable, and uncontrollable. But beneath this façade exists a system that operates with consistency and predictability and, consequently, is subject to control. It is controlling this disorder that is the object of our work. In this book, you will learn how to use behavior therapy to relieve your suffering and have a normal life.

Client education is important in the treatment of many health problems, and it is a critical requirement in the treatment of OCD. This is because *you* are the only one who can eliminate your symptoms. You are your primary therapist and, as such, you must have a comprehensive knowledge of your disorder. This chapter will educate you about the disorder. You will learn what is known about its cause and the specific conditions that are necessary for a formal diagnosis. I'll provide definitions of what obsessions and compulsions are and review some common examples. You'll also be introduced to some other mental and physical activities that can be mistaken for obsessions and compulsions. The chapter ends with a discussion of additional problems generated by OCD, its frequency in the general population, and the path it takes over time, with and without treatment.

A DISORDER OF FEAR

OCD is a disorder of fear—fear of the improbable and the impossible. This book is about one particular type of OCD where washing compulsions are used in futile attempts to offset obsessive fears of being contaminated. These obsessions occur when someone fears they have made contact with substances that are potentially harmful, such as germs, dirt, chemicals, radiation, environmental contaminants, and so forth. This contact activates fear and dread of the possibility of contracting illnesses or fatal diseases. To offset the immediate anxiety and prevent future dreaded outcomes, the person engages in ritualistic washing. This provides some temporary relief but no escape from the grip of endless cycles of contamination obsessions and washing rituals, as Betty's case illustrates.

■ Betty's Fear of Bodily Secretions

Betty, a thirty-two-year-old professional, had managed to successfully graduate high school and complete college, despite having mild to moderate bouts of OCD since childhood. When I started working with her, she had been successfully employed for several years by a large national corporation. However, two years prior to her first visit with me, her obsessive fears intensified. This coincided with her engagement and marriage soon thereafter. She was no longer living alone. This meant she had to reveal her OCD to her husband, Juan, who at first accepted her rituals and avoidances. As time passed her symptoms worsened, and his tolerance for them waned. He urged her to seek treatment, and realizing that her symptoms were getting worse and interfering with their relationship, she did.

Betty had obsessions of being contaminated by urine, blood, and feces. She worried that microscopic particles of one or more of these substances could be on anything that other people touched, which essentially meant just about everything outside her home. Even at home she had problems with things her husband touched if he didn't immediately wash his hands on entering the house. If she touched—or thought she touched—a "contaminated" object or person, she became extremely anxious, feared she would contract AIDS, and washed as soon as possible. When she was clean she knew these fears were ridiculous, but when "contaminated," they seemed real. Frequently she washed "just in case," and estimated washing her hands twenty-five times a day or more.

Washing was always the result of a failure to keep a safe distance from sources she perceived as being contaminated. For example, she wouldn't come within two feet of public waste disposal containers, no matter how elegantly they were designed. Even then she worried about accidental contacts that she hadn't realized at the time, and the uncertainty triggered washing. She diligently tried to avoid touching anything other people touched—from doorknobs to elevator buttons—by asking other people, in public, to open doors or press elevator buttons for her. If nobody was available, she used tissues.

Betty's avoidance behaviors and washing rituals were only partially successful, because she always felt contaminated to some degree outside her home. Nevertheless, she generally managed to complete her day's work. But on those occasions when she touched something that was particularly frightening and washing or using antibacterial hand wipes was mandatory, she was prepared. A stash of wipes was always kept handy. She partially solved the problem of using public toilets by urinating and having bowel movements only at home. Withholding urine for periods of ten to twelve hours or more was an outcome of this practice. Consequently, she had frequent urinary tract infections. Sometimes the pressure to void was greater than her capacity to hold it, and Betty used public toilets by combining the skills of a contortionist and an Olympic gymnast.

Her sanitary sanctuary was her home. And on arriving there, she immediately undressed, put the clothes in the washer, urinated, showered (for 30 minutes or more), and then put on garments worn only in the house. (Betty had tried to get her husband to practice her "decontamination" procedures when he got home, but he refused.) Besides decontaminating herself, she also decontaminated many of the items they brought home. This meant lots of washing of new items before they were used (including new clothes before they were worn), household items, and such. Certain things were impossible to sanitize, so she placed them together in an area set aside for dirty items. When she had to use them, she washed before touching anything else. There were even pieces of furniture she wouldn't sit on, because in her mind they were sources of disease. Recall that for years she lived alone and, over time, developed patterns of avoidance behavior that were practiced daily. So it was predictable that she would try to impose the same patterns of avoidance on her husband. But, similar to his refusal to follow her decontamination practices on entering the house, he refused to comply with her demands to wash his hands before touching this object, sitting in that chair, or using anything that he wanted to use. This was fortunate, because neither of them realized then that joining her in practicing rituals and avoidance would have worsened her symptoms.

However, like most people with OCD, she wanted repeated reassurance that her fears about contamination and illness would not come true. She would constantly ask questions like, "Is this clean? Did you wash your hands? Did I touch that? Did that touch me?" Juan gave her reassurance thinking that he was easing Betty's distress, but ironically the reassurance was harmful. It contributed to the continuation of her symptoms just as it does in all cases of OCD. You'll get a full explanation of how reassurance prevents recovery and how it can be eliminated in chapter 8.

Betty was depressed. Her efforts to cope with her OCD were not working. She became increasingly preoccupied with the fear of being contaminated, which increased the frequency and duration of hand washing, clothes washing, and cleaning of household items. Her conversations with Juan revolved around OCD more than any other topic. At work, intrusive thoughts interfered with her concentration. She felt hopeless.

At this point Betty started behavior therapy and her depression lifted as a result of the elimination of her contamination fears. In addition, there was no further need for compulsive washing and cleaning. This gave her more time and energy to do other things, including engaging in activities and interests with her husband, which strengthened their relationship. She also modified her lifestyle to reduce the possible return of the symptoms. The details of her treatment and methods for preventing relapse will be discussed later.

BEHAVIOR THERAPY, THE TREATMENT OF CHOICE

Referred to as a disorder, OCD is anything but disorderly. The obsessions can be about a variety of thoughts, images, or impulses, and the compulsions can involve any number of repeated actions or thinking patterns. What is most important, however, is not how they look, but how they work. And they always work together, in the same way, in everyone. People have inevitable cycles of irrational fears (*obsessions*) that compel repetitive actions, both mental and physical (*compulsions*, also referred to as *rituals*), which bring relief (See figure 1).

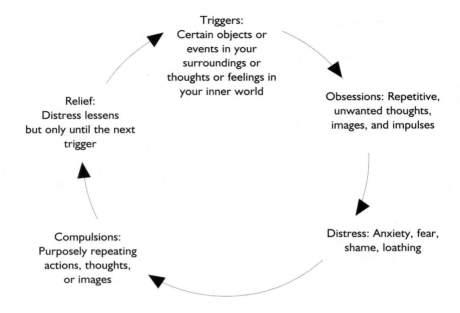

Figure 1: The Obsession-Compulsion Cycle

But this relief lasts only until the onslaught of more irrational fears. This can be a frustrating, vicious cycle, but it's the understanding of this dynamic that enables us to tame the OCD monster. Here's how it works.

The Dynamic

People with OCD develop excessive fears of situations that are not truly dangerous. For example, Betty worried that contact with things that other people touched would contaminate her with microscopic specks of blood that would cause her to develop AIDS. This triggered immediate anxiety and the dread of eventually being HIV-positive. This, in turn, triggered fears of a long period of gruesome illness and ultimately death. These irrational thoughts, which were sometimes accompanied by mental images, were her obsessions. To terminate the immediate anxiety and prevent the long-term dreaded consequences, she washed and cleaned excessively. These behaviors were her compulsions. Once this cycle of obsessions and compulsions is established, it is self-perpetuating and tends to worsen over time.

Taming the OCD Monster

The powerful behavior therapy technique called *exposure and response/ritual prevention* (E&RP), developed by Victor Meyer (1966), breaks this malignant cycle. It eliminates or reduces your obsessions by *desensitizing* you to the fears they provoke. Simply put, the exposure and ritual prevention teaches you to do the opposite of what you have been doing. Instead of avoiding situations that trigger fear, you must expose yourself to them. And instead of engaging in compulsions, you must prevent them. In this way, you will *habituate* to the fear, that is, you simply get used to it. Exposure and response prevention is not as scary as it sounds. To the contrary, it's rewarding, because as you feel the fear gradually falling it tells you that the treatment is working. Also, the exposures are done gradually, which keeps the distress levels in the mild to moderate range.

Once the obsessions have been eliminated, there is, obviously, no need for compulsions. So, to be free of compulsive washing, our first objective will be to free you of the obsessions that trigger washing. You'll learn how to do this in the following chapters.

This kind of exposure therapy works because it relies on the natural ability of the brain to stop responding to thoughts, images, or impulses that are not actually dangerous, which is true of all obsessions. The only requirements are that obsessions be deliberately triggered and the resulting fear not turned off by compulsions. Because the thoughts, images, and impulses are not dangerous, no harm occurs, and the false alarm that the brain previously gave is turned off. Many people wonder why this elimination of the fear has not yet occurred, since they have been exposed to the fear for months or even years. The answer is that people escape from their fears through compulsions and avoidance behaviors, thereby preventing sufficient exposure. But once the fears receive extended and repeated exposure to "the light of day," so to speak, they fade away and can even disappear.

Scientific studies show that these techniques significantly reduce symptoms in 75 percent of those treated (Foa and Kozak 1996). Furthermore, a study my UCLA colleagues and I conducted demonstrated that exposure and response prevention is associated with changes in the brain chemistry of OCD clients that are correlated with reductions in their symptoms (Baxter et al. 1992). For these and other reasons, most experts consider exposure and response prevention the treatment of choice for OCD. It will give you back your life. In addition, you will experience these benefits:

■ Significant reductions or elimination of fear from situations that previously triggered it

■ Few, if any, compulsions

■ No avoidance of situations that were previously troubling

■ Improved mood and self-confidence

■ Higher self-esteem

■ More time and energy for meaningful activities

■ Better personal, social, vocational, and academic functioning

■ The possibility of discontinuing medications

Here are excerpts of comments my patients have made after treatment: "Now I can do more since I stopped taking three or four showers per day," from Sara who had no time for recreational activities. "Notice that I'm wearing a sleeveless blouse," from Noreen who always wore pants and tops with long sleeves that covered her hands to prevent contamination. "See, my hands are looking a lot better," from Tanya whose hands had been red, cracked, and bleeding. "I think I've had my last HIV test," from Jerome who had multiple tests in efforts to quell his fear of AIDS. One of the most touching comments was from a military officer who had a twenty-two-year history of contamination fears: "If it weren't for you, I wouldn't be here. I had decided not to live with OCD."

By fully participating in the treatment program given in this book, you will receive the same benefits as the individuals above and all the others who have learned how to use exposure and response prevention to recover from OCD.

IS THERE ANYONE ELSE LIKE ME?

You are by no means alone. The majority of my clients, at some point in the course of their disorder, have believed they were unique—the only ones afflicted with strange thoughts, anxious feelings, and senseless actions beyond their control. And as much as they'd ponder about the reasons for their condition, they usually drew the wrong conclusions. They would doubt the true nature of their being, and instead dwell on damning self-reprisals that they were inherently contaminated and spreading it, uniquely susceptible to disease, or abnormally irresponsible and careless about hygienic practices. For instance, no matter how much she washed and showered, applied lotions and scents, a meticulous senior accountant never felt really clean and worried about tainting others. Despite excessive washing and showering, a twenty-one-year-old college student could not ease the doubt that he was destined to contract a serious disease. A mother who diligently shielded her children from dangerous contamination she perceived as rampant in public places was convinced that she was not careful and responsible enough. For the people above, great relief followed when they learned they were suffering from a recognized medical condition with symptoms that signified nothing unique about them and that was shared by millions.

Until recently, reliable information on the number of people with OCD was totally lacking. In fact, it was thought that there were few. For instance, the *Diagnostic and Statistical Manual of Mental Disorders*, third edition (1980), reported that "no information" was available on the percentage of people with the disorder. Some estimates did exist, however, which guessed that OCD affected as little as 0.05 percent of the population (Rudin 1953). It wasn't until 1988 that more reliable data, from a survey of 20,500 adults in five cities, determined that at some time during their lives, 2.5 percent of people in the general population will have OCD (Karno et al. 1988). This percentage is fifty times greater than the previous estimates and means that, at any one time, over seven million people in the United States have or will have the disorder. This high frequency is two to three times higher than that of bipolar disorder (manic depressive illness), panic disorder, or schizophrenia.

Since approximately one of every forty people has OCD, it is quite possible that you have encountered a number of people with the condition. Exactly who, you do not know, due to the fact that most people with OCD keep it to themselves. Consider the probability that in a typical high school of two thousand students, approximately fifty students would have the problem. In a university of twenty thousand students, there would be four to five hundred. And in a city the size of Sacramento, California, there would be eight to nine thousand. So, you can see that you are by no means alone.

WHEN IT STARTS AND WHERE IT GOES

Studies show that OCD in adults usually starts in a person's early twenties (Antony, Downie, and Swinson 1998). In a study of thirty-one children and adolescents suffering from OCD, 29 percent of subjects reported that they developed symptoms at the age seven or less, 52 percent at the ages of eight to twelve, and 19 percent at ages thirteen and above (Hanna 1995). Several studies have shown that the occurrence of symptoms after the age of fifty is rare (Ingram 1961; Jenike 1991; Kolada, Bland, and Newman 1994).

Based on their experience, most mental-health practitioners have the impression that, without treatment, OCD tends to wax and wane over time. Rasmussen and Tsuang studied the course of the disorder in forty-four clients and found that 84 percent had no change in their condition, 14 percent worsened, and 2 percent had an up-and-down course. They also found that these patients, on the average, waited about seven and a half years to seek treatment after having their first symptoms (1986).

In the study, 25 percent could point to a specific stressful event just before the onset of their OCD, while 75 percent could not. Typical stresses included an increase in responsibility (like work or study overload) or a loss of some kind (like a death of a loved one or the loss of a job). Almost all the subjects believed that stress intensified their symptoms. For some women, the stress of pregnancy can acti-vate OCD symptoms. In one group of fifty-nine mothers with OCD, 39 percent reported that the disorder started during pregnancy (Neziroglu, Anemone, and Yaryura-Tobias 1992).

The significance of all these numbers is that OCD can strike a person early in life and, without treatment, will most likely persist. Although some can identify specific stressful events for its onset, most people cannot. Once OCD is present, however, almost all agree that life stresses worsen the symptoms. Probably the most important facts are that the disorder will not go away of its own accord, and that you can learn to significantly decrease or eliminate your symptoms and have a normal life.

WHY DOES IT HAPPEN?

We don't really know what causes OCD, but we do know what does not cause it. OCD is not due to flaws of character, such as moral or spiritual weakness or lack of courage. OCD is not a punishment for past actions or inactions for which you feel guilty. And there is no good evidence that faulty child-rearing methods, toilet training in particular, cause the condition. Furthermore, it is not a result of your irrational thinking. There are, however, mental health professionals who do believe that it is. Therefore to eliminate or reduce symptoms, these therapists attempt to teach the client to entertain rational thoughts to replace irrational ones. Not only does this technique fail, it can teach you new mental rituals that offer only a temporary relief and increase obsessions in the long run.

Psychodynamic Explanations

One of the oldest theories suggests OCD is the result of psycho-logical conflicts of which the individual is unaware. Therapists who hold this view believe that obsessions, because of their persistence, serve to block other more painful ideas from coming into a person's awareness. These painful ideas are usually unacceptable thoughts or urges of an aggressive or sexual nature that are in conflict with the person's values. Therapists of this school of thought believe that if clients can develop insight into the existence and nature of the repressed conflict, it will be resolved and the obsessions will disappear. This type of treatment, variously called psychoanalysis, psychodynamic, traditional, or insight-oriented psychotherapy, has not been shown to be effective for OCD (Esman 2001). The most likely reason is that OCD is not caused by repressed psychological conflicts, but by problems with brain functioning.

The Chemical Superhighway—Serotonin

OCD may be associated with insufficient levels of *serotonin,* a brain chemical necessary for the transmission of information across brain cells. Support for this possibility comes from the improvement seen in OCD patients after they've taken drugs that increase the availability of serotonin. It has also been observed that people with OCD have abnormally high metabolic rates in certain areas of their brains, which tend to decrease following treatment with either behavior therapy or medications (Baxter et al. 1992).

All in the Family—Genetics

Genetic factors also appear to play a role. People with OCD have a significantly higher percentage of parents, siblings, and offspring with the disorder than people who do not have the disorder. Also, the frequency of OCD occurring in each identical twin is two times greater than OCD occurring in each unidentical twin (Billett, Richter, and Kennedy 1998).

Strep Infection—PANDAS

In certain children, OCD symptoms emerge or are worsened during cases of strep throat. Research into the cause of this has led to speculation that the antibodies that fight the strep infection also attack nerve tissue in the basal ganglia of the brain. This results in OCD or tic symptoms. Susan Swedo, a behavioral pediatrician, has labeled this Pediatric Autoimmune Neuropsychiatric Disorder Associated with Strep (PANDAS). In cases where the onset of OCD or tic symptoms is sudden or dramatically worsened, strep infections should be considered. Medical treatments with antibiotics may benefit some of these patients (Swedo, Leonard, and Kiessling 1994).

Behavioral Explanations

For unknown reasons, the fear system in the brain sends false alarms of danger when it processes certain thoughts, images, or urges that most people simply ignore. For others, however, the thoughts persist and become triggers for intense fear bordering on terror, eventually becoming obsessions. Instinctively, the person tries to avoid these triggers, but this is impossible because triggers are everywhere. Thus, when contact is made, the victims somehow acquire the habit of using certain repetitive actions or mental activities that become compulsions used to get relief, albeit temporarily. From then on, they rely on compulsions and avoidance to cope with the fear. Adding even more anguish to the fear is the person's knowledge that it is unreasonable. "Why do I still react this way when I know it doesn't make sense?" they ask. They don't understand that reason alone is powerless in the face of irrational fear. Only direct confrontation through exposure to fear quiets the brain's fear system and stops the false alarms.

Biobehavioral Explanations

Many people who study OCD view it as the result of a combination of biological and psychological responses to the inevitable stresses of life. People with OCD report that pressures from ordinary life events frequently preceded the onset of their symptoms. Even "positive" stresses such as graduating from school, moving, getting married, being promoted, having a baby, and so forth, have been associated with the appearance of symptoms. Psychological and physical trauma also seem to be a frequent precursor of the disorder. At UCLA, we observed that 30 percent of the chronic OCD client population had been victims of sexual, physical, or psychological trauma (Bystritsky et al. 1996). So it is plausible to consider that the cause of OCD may involve a combination of biological and environmental events. It seems that, when there is a biological predisposition for the disorder, the symptoms can manifest when sufficient environmental stress triggers them.

But enough of this theoretical talk, because even though we do not fully understand the causes of this disorder, we know enough about how it works to treat it. But first, let's discuss what's required for the diagnosis of OCD. Obviously the person must have obsessions and compulsions. Although each person's OCD has features that are unique to the person, there are several combinations of obsessions and compulsions that commonly occur. Let's take a look at them.

ABOUT OBSESSIONS AND COMPULSIONS

Obsessions are defined as recurrent and persistent thoughts, impulses, or images that are intrusive. They are inappropriate and persistent, and cause extreme anxiety or distress. Obsessions are not merely excessive worries about real life problems, but instead, they are anxieties about the occurrence of highly unlikely or totally unrealistic events. (A good example of this was Betty's realization that her obsessions of contracting AIDS from door handles was ridiculous.) The person realizes that the obsessions are caused by their own mind. Many people and mental-health professionals commonly refer to obsessions as worries or fears. In fact, the word "fear" is used synonymously with "obsession," because once the obsession starts, it instantaneously activates the fear response.

Compulsions are repetitive actions or mental activities that a person feels compelled to do following an obsession. The person thinks these activities will reduce distress or prevent something bad from happening. Frequently, they are excessive and not realistically connected to what they are designed to neutralize. Betty's washing activity illustrated this. As mentioned earlier, compulsions are frequently referred to as rituals.

Frequently Occurring Obsessions and Their Compulsions

There are several types of obsessions that are quite common and trigger certain compulsions. Even though our focus in this book is on fears of being contaminated that lead to compulsive washing, it is good for you to be aware of other frequently associated obsessions and compulsions. Many of you may have more than one of them.

Obsessions about being irresponsible or careless → Checking compulsions. People with these obsessions are plagued by excessive and unreasonable doubts about safely and competently performing many routine activities of daily living, such as locking doors, turning off stoves, paying bills, and even driving. They will repeatedly check to be sure things were done correctly or that they have not unintentionally harmed someone. Yet for many, fear of blame or criticism for imagined negligence persists even though people with this form of OCD are far more careful and accident free than most of us.

Harm obsessions → Repeating compulsions. This type involves thoughts, impulses, or images of hurting others. A mother has images of killing her infant. A newlywed has thoughts of stabbing her sleeping husband. A young boy fears turning into a vampire and attacking his parents. These obsessions cause worries about being homicidal, going berserk, or even becoming a serial killer. Those of you with harm obsessions can take comfort in knowing that there are no known cases of people with OCD carrying out their harmful thoughts.

When people have harming thoughts or images, they may repeat whatever activity they were doing when the thought occurred, while trying to replace it with a good thought. They may repeatedly turn lights on and off, go back and forth through doorways, or tap themselves or objects. The repetitions are frequently carried out with counting.

Sexual obsessions → Compulsive confessing and reassurance seeking. These are unwanted persistent thoughts, images, or impulses of engaging in inappropriate sexual activities. A heterosexual man who regards homosexuality as unacceptable fears he is really gay. A son has images of sexual activity with his mother. A young woman will not allow people into her home because she fears she would lose control and have sex with them.

Confessing and seeking reassurance are common compulsions for coping with sexual obsessions. The person will tell a significant other of their unwanted sexual obsessions, and will seek reassurance that they won't carry out a perverse act or that they aren't a bad person. Mentally going over reasons why his or her fear won't materialize is common.

Blasphemous obsessions → Praying and confessing compulsions.
The obsessions are about thoughts, images, or impulses that are sacrilegious or against God and/or religion. Typically, such obsessions occur in those who are truly religious. Often their presence causes grave doubts and even worries of being possessed.

Mental compulsions of praying, making religious gestures, and repeating certain phrases in a ritualistic way are common attempts people make to deal with blasphemous obsessions. Confessing and reassurance seeking are also prevalent.

Obsessions of losing or discarding something important → Hoarding.
These obsessions cause people to fear that they might throw away something that is important, that they might need in the future, or that is in some way worthwhile. Consequently, they compulsively accumulate unneeded objects—old newspapers and magazines, receipts, unused clothing, aluminum cans, used food containers, and so on—to the point where the hoarded material occupies too much of their living space.

Obsessions about symmetry and orderliness → Arranging and ordering compulsions. With this type, the person has intense anxiety when objects are not symmetrical or precisely arranged. He or she must hang shirts in the closet according to color, exactly equidistant from each other; objects on desks, tables, and other surfaces are placed in certain arrangements that must always be maintained; and footprints in the carpet are immediately smoothed out. Visitors to the person's home are not welcomed because they will inevitably disturb things and make work for the host who has to put everything back just as it was. The compulsions used to ameliorate the anxiety are to immediately put objects in their "correct" order.

Unique obsessions → Unique compulsions. This category includes a host of obsessions that are highly unique to the individual. For example, a patient of mine feared that if she noticed things that caused her to think of blindness, that her daughter would go blind. To prevent this, she relied on a compulsion of immediately showering, even though she was fully aware of the lack of relevance of this behavior to preventing blindness. This is but one example of what are probably tens of thousands of unique obsessions.

People with OCD frequently look for examples of their particular form of the disorder in hopes of finding out that it was successfully treated. If they can't find an example of an obsession-compulsion combination like theirs, they feel discouraged. Don't be. Even frequently occurring obsessions and compulsions have unique features that vary from person to person. It is not what the obsessions and compulsions look like that is important, but how they work. Regardless of their form, obsessions are always about something that is highly unlikely or impossible yet provokes fear, and the compulsions are always some kind of excessive or inappropriate mental or physical action that temporarily reduces fear. Psychologists have discovered ways to treat OCD by disrupting this relationship, so the OCD disintegrates. I'll teach you how to do this in the chapters to come.

ACCORDING TO THE BOOK

Mental health professionals rely on the *Diagnostic and Statistical Manual of Mental Disorders,* fourth edition, known as the DSM-IV (American Psychiatric Association 1994). This manual is used in diagnosing various mental conditions. The conditions necessary for the diagnosis of OCD are as follows.

Condition A. According to the DSM-IV, the person must have either obsessions or compulsions. However, all of the patients I've treated have had both obsessions and compulsions. This leads me to believe that they always work in combination.

Condition B. The person must recognize that their obsessions and compulsions are unrealistic and excessive. If most of the time the person does not recognize his or her obsessions or compulsions as excessive or unreasonable, then their diagnosis is given the additional specification of "with poor insight." This means they believe their fears are real, and their compulsions protect them from distress or something bad happening.

Condition C. The obsessions or compulsions must cause significant distress, consume a total time of more than one hour per day, or significantly interfere with the person's occupational, educational, or social activities.

Condition D. The disorder is not considered OCD if there are obsessions or compulsions about food in a person with an eating disorder; hair pulling as a result of trichotillomania; excessive and inappropriate concern with appearance due to body dysmorphic disorder; preoccupation with drugs because of a substance use disorder; preoccupation with having a serious illness because of hypochondriasis; excessive sexual urges or fantasies due to paraphilia (intense sexual activity or desires involving unusual objects, activities, or situations); or guilty ruminations due to a major depressive disorder.

Condition E. The obsessions or compulsions are not a result of a substance, such as drugs of abuse, medications, or a general medical condition (like hyper- and hypothyroidism).

IT'S NOT ABOUT LOVE

It's worth discussing what OCD is not, since the words "obsession" and "compulsion" have meanings in everyday usage that are different from their use in OCD. When people say someone has an obsession about something, they usually mean that he or she has a fascination, preoccupation, fancy, or passion for it in the same way the person loves something or somebody. This is a positive state of affairs, and the person's behavior is under his or her own control. For example, when a young man finally meets the young woman of his dreams and finds that he cannot stop thinking about her, he is basking in the rapture of love, not trapped in the hellish prison of fearful, repetitive thoughts.

Obsessions should not be confused with symptoms of a major depressive episode or generalized anxiety disorder. In a major depressive disorder, the person is usually voluntarily engrossed in thoughts of self-worthlessness and guilt about past actions. In contrast, obsessions are involuntary and are concerned with dreaded future consequences. In generalized anxiety disorder, there is excessive worry about real-life circumstances, whereas obsessions are always focused on the unlikely or fantastic. Most people with OCD recognize the unreasonableness of their obsessions, except when they're in the agony of them, at which time they may believe them. If, however, they are always convinced that their fear is real, then they are most likely suffering from delusional disorder.

The word "compulsion" also has a different meaning when used in an everyday sense as opposed to its OCD meaning. A woman may regularly clear her desk before leaving work and never fail to carefully wash her hands before preparing food. These actions are not necessarily compulsions if she finds satisfaction in them, and they do not interfere with the smooth flow of her life. Even the behaviors of excessive overeating, gambling, drinking, drug taking, smoking, sexual activity, and a variety of other bad habits are not considered compulsions, because people find them pleasurable and they are not triggered by obsessions.

Two additional conditions sometimes confused with compulsions are tic disorder and stereotypic movement disorder. In tic disorder, the person makes unexpected, rapid, repeated movements or vocalizations. Examples are eye blinking, tongue thrusting, and throat clearing. In stereotypic movement disorder, there are actions such as head banging, body rocking, and self-biting. Tics and stereotyped movements differ from compulsions because they are less complicated and not aimed at neutralizing obsessions. However, people can have symptoms of OCD, tic disorder, and stereotypic movement disorder at the same time.

AND IF THAT'S NOT ENOUGH

People with OCD frequently have other emotional and behavioral conditions, the most common being depression and other anxiety disorders (Antony, Downie, and Swinson 1998).

Depression

Two studies found that approximately 30 percent of the OCD patients studied met the conditions of a major depressive episode (Karno et al. 1988; Yaryura-Tobias et al. 1996). This means they had five or more of the following symptoms nearly every day over a two-week period:

- Depressed mood most of the day

- Loss of interest or pleasure

- Significant weight loss or gain, or decrease or increase in appetite

- Insomnia

- Restlessness or slowness

- Fatigue or loss of energy

- Feelings of worthlessness or guilt

- Difficulty thinking, concentrating, or making decisions

- Recurrent thoughts of death, suicidal thoughts with or without a specific plan, or a suicide attempt

The above symptoms must have caused significant distress or impairment in important areas of life and not be due to drug abuse, medication, or grieving the loss of a loved one.

Many people with OCD are clinically depressed, frequently as a result of the OCD, and once the OCD improves, the depression lifts. However, if the depression is severe, it can interfere with OCD treatment because one needs energy and concentration to complete the exercises that are part of behavior therapy. In such cases, it is probably best to address the depression first and then, after there is improvement, treat the OCD.

Anxiety Disorders

It is not unusual for OCD sufferers to have other anxiety disorders, most commonly social phobia, specific phobia, panic disorder, and generalized anxiety disorder (Antony, Downie, and Swinson 1998).

- In social phobia, the person has an irrational fear of doing something embarrassing or being criticized when around other people.

- In specific phobia, there is a persistent, unreasonable fear, triggered by an object or situation (like flying, heights, animals, receiving an injection, seeing blood).

- In panic disorder, there are repeated attacks of unexpected, intense fear, accompanied by a number of bodily sensations of physical arousal, which causes people to fear they are having a heart attack, going crazy, or losing control.

- In generalized anxiety disorder, people worry excessively and are anxious about everyday life concerns of income, health, family, job, or education.

The presence of these anxiety disorders, which are also quite responsive to behavior therapy, does not necessarily preclude treating the OCD. The question is which should be treated first, or whether the anxiety disorders should be treated along with the OCD.

Reading about the above conditions might have caused some of you to worry that you have one of them and didn't realize it until now. If so, take comfort in knowing that these mood and anxiety disorders are quite responsive to treatment, just as OCD is. Also, you may be concerned that receiving a diagnosis of one of these disorders will cause you to be "labeled." I too find it objectionable when diagnoses are used as labels to classify people disapprovingly, for example, calling those with OCD "obsessives" or "compulsives." This has the effect of reducing a person to a mental disorder rather than regarding them as a human being with a disorder. However, there is considerable value in knowing and using the correct name for what ails you. These labels provide a framework for organizing our thinking so that problems can be systematically attacked and good treatment outcomes produced. Furthermore, some of these conditions exist, at some time to some degree, in most of us. You may be surprised to know that as much as 80 percent of the population experiences unpleasant, intrusive thoughts similar to obsessions (Rachman and De Silva 1978), and 55 percent performs compulsions (Muris, Merckelbach, and Clavan 1997). However, so-called "normal" obsessions and compulsions are less frequent, intense, and of shorter duration than those of OCD. It's when the level of distress interferes with your life flow that you should regard the condition as needing professional attention.

Summary

With the information you have acquired from reading this chapter, you know at least as much about OCD as many mental-health professionals do, and more than some. Also, you should have a good idea about whether you have OCD. You have taken the first step toward your recovery. In the next chapter, we will examine the contamination-washing cycle, and by understanding how it works you will learn how to take it apart.

CHAPTER 2

Contamination Fears and Other Triggers

Now that you have been introduced to the way OCD works and how it's treated, we'll focus on the specific problem this book will help you solve—compulsive washing. We'll do this by examining a repeating cycle of triggers that follow one another as systematically as do the seasons of the year and phases of the moon. By understanding the way it works, psychologists have devised strategies for disrupting this cycle and the symptoms it maintains. You'll learn these strategies in chapters to come.

But first, you may wonder why you have washing rituals and not, say, checking rituals. So before dissecting the contamination and washing cycle, here are some speculations on why people have the OCD subtypes they have.

WHY WASHING COMPULSIONS?

As you know by now, there are several subtypes of OCD. So what is it about the disorder that causes a person to have the subtype that they have? Why does Bill have washing rituals, Mary checking rituals, and Joe repeating rituals? Is there something about each person that determines the type of obsessive fear that activates their particular rituals? We'll have to wait for a careful scientific investigation to answer this question definitively. However, in the meantime, I offer the following speculations.

People with washing compulsions have probably had frightening experiences associated with contamination that have caused them to fear anything of questionable cleanliness. This kind of sensitivity can also result from observing or hearing about someone with an illness or injury that might have been caused by contamination. It's also reasonable to speculate that there are those who have taken too much to heart such teachings as "cleanliness is next to godliness." The following cases are examples of *conditioning events* (traumatic experiences associated with contamination) that led to contamination obsessions and washing rituals.

■ Judith's Story: The Fear of Death

When she was about six or seven, an aunt with terminal cancer came to live with Judith and her family. Judith was afraid that touching her aunt would cause cancer, so she diligently avoided any contact with her. The aunt eventually chose a winged back chair as her favorite and sat in it frequently, which, in Judith's mind, contaminated it with cancer germs. Eventually even the sight of it frightened her. The aunt also sat on other furniture, used objects in the home, and had physical contact with people, all of whom became contaminated in Judith's view.

By the time Judith saw see me for treatment, she was in her mid-fifties, and her contamination fears had spread to everything outside her apartment. However, she could tolerate contamination in the outside world, knowing that when she returned home she would immediately remove her clothes and place them in a special container by the door to be scrupulously washed later. Then she would wash her entire body with alcohol to purify herself from all the germs from the outside world. After that she was "comfy." Judith had practiced these compulsions for over thrity years during which time she had a rewarding career and even successfully raised, as a single mother, a son. Although he wasn't made to bathe in alcohol, he followed his mother's rituals of removing his clothes on coming home and immediately taking a shower. Remarkably, coming up in this environment seemed to have no harmful effects on him as he did well academically, professionally, and socially. He was married, had a son, and practiced normal hygienic routines.

To keep her apartment clean, it was off-limits to everyone except her son and, eventually, her grandson. On one occasion, repairs had to be made, and a serviceman came in to do them. She said that it took her weeks to restore her place to its pure state. One reason she was seeking treatment was prompted by seeing paramedics in the lobby of her apartment building taking a man on a stretcher to their ambulance. She guessed he had suffered a heart attack, and the paramedics had been in his apartment. This started worrying her about her own heart disease and, in the event of an emergency, paramedics contaminating her apartment. This would mean weeks of cleaning. (It struck me that she was more concerned about the cleaning rituals than the consequences of a heart attack.) Another reason was that her three-year-old grandson, who periodically made overnight visits, had started asking questions about her washing rituals that she was finding difficult to answer. Furthermore, she did not want him to participate in her practices the way that her son had. Finally, after several years of psychodynamic psychotherapy that had no effect on her OCD symptoms, she wanted to try behavior therapy.

Judith's story illustrates the way we can automatically learn to become fearful of things through conditioning. It started when Aunt Alice moved in with the family. A niece would typically welcome this event, but for Judith, her aunt provoked fear of cancer and death. This fear became associated with the aunt's favorite chair, and eventually just the sight of the chair itself provoked fear. She had become conditioned to fear the chair. However, the conditioning does not stop with just one association of a previously neutral situation with a fear. It continues to change more and more neutral situations into feared ones. Recall that the aunt also sat on other furniture, used objects in the home, and made contact with people, all of which became triggers for fear. You can see that a kind of conditioned fear contagion happens that eventually results in many situations, events, circumstances, people, etc. eventually becoming fear triggers. Most people with OCD are aware that the number of situations they find difficult have increased over time, even though they may be unaware of the original event that conditioned their fear of them.

The following story is yet another example of the way that fearful events can shape the content of obsessions. It differs from Judith's story in that the conditioning event was an outrageous instance of child abuse.

■ Betty's Story: That Word

Betty was about five or six, playing with a friend in the living room, when she said "shit." Her father, who was outside, heard her, rushed in, grabbed her by the arm, and yanked her out into the yard. There he picked up a piece of dog stool and stuffed it in her mouth while yelling, "I don't want to hear you say that word ever again!" Crying, Betty ran into the house and washed her mouth out with soap and water. (As you'll recall, Betty is the woman we met in chapter 1 who had fears of bodily secretions.) Does it seem logical to conclude that there might have been a connection between that traumatic event and the contamination obsessions and washing rituals that eventually developed?

The above case examples are illustrations of the possible association between traumatic events and the eventual subtypes of OCD that occur. They are not offered as examples of *causes* for OCD. As discussed in chapter 1, the disorder seems to be primarily a result of biological and genetic factors, with environmental events contributing to its onset and the particular form the OCD takes. Furthermore, many people cannot recall any specific traumatic events that were associated with their subtype. More importantly, this information isn't necessary for successful treatment. If it is proven that there is an association between traumas and OCD subtypes, it will be further evidence that conditioning is a major factor in the development of obsessive fears in general and their content in particular. Regardless of its origin, once compulsive washing is established, its cycle of operation is the same from person to person regardless of their differences.

Now let's examine the seemingly endless cycles of fear, rituals, and temporary relief.

THE CONTAMINATION-WASHING CYCLE: A CHAIN REACTION

The contamination-washing cycle is a chain reaction of triggers that works like this:

1. **Something in your inner or outer world triggers obsessions.** You have thoughts about dirt or germs, or your senses react to something in your surroundings that seems contaminated. In either case, you are bombarded by the thoughts, images, or impulses of unrelenting obsessions.

2. **The obsessions trigger fear.** The obsessions trigger instantaneous fear, anxiety, disgust, shame, and any number of other terrible emotions. You have dread and worry about something bad happening at some unknown future time. Try as you might, you can't dismiss these distressful feelings.

3. **The fear triggers rituals.** You engage in washing compulsions, and in some cases, mental compulsions. There can also be the hope that the compulsions will prevent illness, disease, or other dreaded consequences.

4. **The rituals trigger relief.** The anguish from the obsessions subsides temporarily. Though you may experience fatigue from energy spent ritualizing and humiliation from practicing senseless behaviors, the rituals eventually become automatic whenever triggers are encountered.

5. **The cycle ends.** As you know, the relief is short-lived because triggers are everywhere and unavoidable, so recurring contamination cycles are inevitable. The more they are performed, the stronger they become, and the weaker your will to resist them.

TRIGGERS FOR OBSESSIONS

The contamination-washing cycle starts when you notice something in your environment or your mind that triggers obsessions. Triggers for most people are related to potential health hazards from dirt or germs to toxic substances. However, for some, the triggers are unique, and the person's washing compulsions have no practical relationship to the fears they are trying to relieve. We'll review both types of these fear activators in the following section.

Common Triggers Associated with Contamination

Most people with compulsive washing say that it is triggered by dirt or germs commonly found in certain bodily substances and on objects other people touch. For others, chemicals, radiation, and environmental contaminants are seen as untouchable. In this section, I'll describe these commonly perceived contaminants that provoke avoidance and compulsive washing. Some of you may find it difficult to read the following list of words and the rest of the material in this section. The subject matter may trigger discomfort and the impulse to skip it. If your reaction is strong enough, you may even feel like washing your hands after touching these pages. If this is true, repeatedly reading this section can work as an exposure exercise that will help to desensitize you to your contamination fears and help you to resist excessive washing. The underlying principles for doing so are given in chapter 4. However, if your reaction is more than you can bear, pass over this section for now and read the rest of the chapter starting with the heading "Fears Triggered by Obsessions."

Bodily Substances

People who fear these substances find their own bodies to be a source of their distress, which they must confront daily.

Feces. The fear of germs from feces is widespread partly because people with OCD notice that there are people who don't wash their hands after using public restrooms and are, therefore, spreading it to objects that everybody touches. The fear persists despite the fact that they have never seen feces on anything they avoid. When confronted with this lack of evidence, they say that the feces and germs are there, but in microscopic specks, invisible to the naked eye. Or, they can fear random brown spots and objects similar in shape and color to both human and animal excrement, and will stay away from them. In fact, presenting those who are highly sensitive with a smudge of brown shoe polish on a tissue will frighten them and trigger washing just as if it were the real thing. This happens even when I show people the bottle of shoe polish and smudge the tissue while they're watching. It's a good demonstration of fear overriding reason, which is at the core of OCD.

Urine. This is also widely feared as a transporter of germs, even though urine is sterile. And like feces, people with OCD worry that it is on just about everything, in microscopic amounts, that people touch. Other liquids that resemble urine, like the example above given with feces, can also trigger obsessions and compulsive washing.

Blood. Although encountered less frequently than the above two substances, fear of blood is common, largely due to worries about HIV infection, sexually transmitted diseases, and other serious illnesses. Again, no visible evidence of it is necessary to provoke obsessions and compulsions, because those who fear it believe it's in bodily substances, the air, on surfaces, and almost everywhere. Red food coloring, ink smudges, paint drippings, and the like, even when recognized as such by the person, will provoke OCD reactions.

Saliva. For some, saliva is yet another means by which germs and diseases are spread. It is particularly disrupting when the fear reaches a level that interferes with personal relationships. Consider the sufferer who must maintain socially awkward distances from people when having face-to-face conversations. Worrying about spittle, he finds it hard to focus on what's being said, and the speaker is put off by talking to a person who seems to be on the verge of taking his leave at any moment. Consider the young woman who could not enjoy the pleasure of a kiss until her husband first brushed his teeth and gargled three times. She would also make up reasons to leave for work before he was awake so she could avoid the goodbye kiss. Before more intimate relations, he had to shower three times. Don't let anyone sneeze, because this will surely cause a hasty retreat to a sanctuary where the sufferer will ritualize to prevent something bad from happening. The dreaded fears that saliva triggers range from catching colds or the flu to contracting AIDS or cancer.

Semen. Despite the fact that semen is found only in intimate sexual situations, the fear of it, and substances that resemble it, abound. Mayonnaise, salad dressings, melted ice cream, tapioca pudding, hairdressings, Elmer's glue, and as many things as you can imagine are avoided because of what they look like. Items associated with sex and consequently semen are feared as well. The number of used condoms, disposed of in public places, which are spotted by people with this fear is remarkable. Nevertheless, contact with, or even being near, semen, its look-alikes, and things associated with sex can trigger anxieties about illness and a fear of pregnancy even without the benefit of intercourse.

Toxic Substances

Substances and materials that are potentially poisonous provoke excessive fear, avoidance, and rituals in people with obsessions of harm.

Chemicals. The fear of harm from chemicals typically involves cleansers, solvents, insecticides, fertilizers, deodorants, and other compounds and solutions frequently found in the home. People with these fears will avoid them or take elaborate precautions when they or others are using them. Contact can cause uncomfortable physical sensations, high anxiety, panic, and fear of eventual serious illnesses. If contact occurs, the dire consequences are defended against with compulsive washing.

Medications. Fear of prescription and over-the-counter medications occurs much too frequently in people with contamination fears. This is but another one of OCD's many ironies. That is, medications that can relieve OCD symptoms, such as SSRIs (selective serotonin reuptake inhibitors), can trigger obsessions and the refusal to take them. This kind of avoidance can not only delay recovery from OCD, but can have lethal consequences for those who need other medications for life-threatening illnesses.

Environmental Contaminants

Information about increasing threats to the purity of our air, water, and soil exacerbate the already high anxiety of people with these concerns.

Trash. These triggers include garbage, litter, rubbish, junk, and their containers. Seen as hotbeds of filth and breeding grounds for germs, people with these fears will refuse to take out the garbage, walk by public trash containers, or drive by dumpsters. Certain people, who would be considered by most standards as dirty, are also triggers. But like beauty, filth and grime is in the eye of the beholder who has contamination fears. This means a person's actual state of dishevelment or griminess doesn't necessarily define them as contaminated. People generally considered dirty may or may not be a threat, while those who are appropriately groomed and dressed may be. In either case, simply being close to any of the above threats, let alone brushing against them, results in washing rituals that can last for hours.

Radiation. Microwave ovens, cell phones, X-rays, neon lights, copiers, computers, and other electronic equipment trigger fears of genetic damage, skin disease, tumors, cancer, and other mental and physical disorders in those sensitized to these triggers. There are, however, reasonable concerns about the possible long-term health problems posed by these devices. So how can you know if your fear is irrational, as it is in OCD, or reasonable, based on the thoughtful evaluation of available information? The answer is given by your emotional and behavioral responses following contact with the potential hazard. If you immediately react with high anxiety that compels washing and avoidance activities that are life-interfering, then it's most likely OCD.

Metals. Mercury and lead are truly toxic when ingested in sufficient amounts over time. However, they're so diligently dodged by those who fear them that their health risks are nil. Yet their avoidance offers no comfort. They constantly feel threatened by these metals, seeing them everywhere. One person I worked with wouldn't use pencils because he thought they contained lead. When I explained that the pencil marks were from graphite and not lead, he said he believed me but adamantly refused to hold one. Like lead, the presence of mercury is universal in the worldview of the fearful. They know it's used in thermometers, thermostats, batteries, advertising signs, paint, antiseptics, dental fillings, and even more things than I know about. Ironically, this knowledge is not helpful but burdensome, for it renders the knower excessively vigilant and avoidant, disrupting the normal flow of their lives.

Atmospheric pollutants. Gases from home fireplaces and furnaces, power generation, and motor vehicles pollute the air. They are suspected or known to be harmful, and this information is widely circulated by the news media. This is bad news we all agree, but most of us, feeling powerless to do anything about it, shrug it off. But not those whose obsessions focus on atmospheric contaminants. They are constantly aware of vehicle emissions, smog, gasoline vapors, smoke, and other toxins. They attempt to cope by using avoidance as their first line of defense. They avoid driving on freeways, pumping gas, frequenting smoky restaurants and bars, and steer clear of other toxic situations. When avoidance doesn't work, the person relies on washing rituals as the second line of defense to relieve distress and prevent bad things from happening.

Triggers Unrelated to Contamination

People and situations that have nothing to do with dirt, germs, or disease can activate obsessive fears that compel washing rituals. This section covers some of these triggers starting with those that are fairly common and concluding with those that are less common.

Sticky and greasy substances. Sticky foods such as jams, chocolate bars, caramels, and sweet rolls and items such as adhesive tape, labels, and glue can trigger compulsive washing, not because of contamination fears, but because of distressing skin sensations. Greasy substances and objects can cause the same disagreeable feelings. People so affected say that there's something on their hands they can't see but can vividly feel. The physical sensations are also accompanied by strong anxiety that drives washing rituals.

People. Washing compulsions can be triggered by fears that have to do with emotions or sensations triggered by noncontaminated people and conditions. These triggers are usually associated with the feared content of the sufferer's obsessions. For example, those with violent obsessions may wash their hands when someone makes them angry, believing that the ritual will prevent them from losing control and lashing out. Some who have obsessions of unacceptable sexual activity say their fears are triggered and they feel "contaminated" when they are around people who are the objects of their sexual obsessions. To diminish distress and prevent "bad things from happening," they will resort to hand washing, showering, or other cleaning rituals. These are but two examples of the many ways that compulsions become rituals of choice, even though they have no purposeful connection to the fears they temporarily allay.

Unique triggers. These are triggers that seem to affect only a single individual, that appear to be one of a kind. For example, I treated a man who had anxiety bordering on panic whenever he saw or heard fire engines, firefighters, or anything related to fire departments. He tried to cope by avoiding firehouses, covering his ears at the first sound of sirens, and closing his eyes when he spotted firefighting equipment or personnel. Even red cars and trucks caused his heart rate and breathing to increase. When he panicked and feared that he was going crazy, he immediately stopped at the first place that had a public restroom and washed. Although it gave relief, the ritual embarrassed him because of its absurd, irrelevant connection to the fear.

Another person endured intense anxiety when he saw actors in movies who later committed suicide in real life. Seeing them on film caused fear that he would commit suicide if he didn't ritualistically wash his hands and clean his kitchen. He was at a loss to explain the origin of the fear or its connection to washing.

I worked with a woman who was compelled to avoid all things associated with blindness, because failure to do so would cause her daughter to go blind. This meant not hearing, seeing, or having physical contact with people, objects, or situations even remotely related to blindness. For example, she didn't use elevators because the buttons for selecting floors were numbered in braille. Since complete avoidance was impossible and she made occasional contact with some forms of the threat, she would immediately shower to prevent her daughter's loss of sight. The urgency to perform this ritual was so powerful that when fear was triggered away from her apartment, she immediately rushed home and started showering while dressed.

All of the people in the above examples learned to overcome their symptoms, just as you will be able to, by practicing exercises you'll learn in the following chapters.

FEARS TRIGGERED BY OBSESSIONS

The above contamination obsessions instantaneously trigger fears of dreaded consequences. The following consequences are common:

- Fear of anxiety or panic attacks

- Fear of skin irritations

- Fear of illness and disease

- Fear of spreading contamination

- Fear of contaminating others

Anxiety, Panic, Going Crazy

Many people with contamination fears do not worry about illness from contamination but are afraid of the unending high anxiety and panic attacks from exposure to it. They come to believe that only washing compulsively will stop their distress. They become extremely sensitive to any of the symptoms of high anxiety or panic. Many people are not sure of the difference between a panic attack and high anxiety. It's a panic attack when you have fear or discomfort and four or more of the following physical reactions. It's high anxiety if you have less than four of the following reactions:

- Pounding heart or quickened heart rate

- Sweating

- Numbness or tingling

- Chills or hot flashes

- Trembling or shaking

- Shortness of breath or feelings of smothering

- Choking sensations

- Chest pain, discomfort, or fear of a heart attack

- Abdominal distress or nausea

- Feeling dizzy, unsteady, faint, or light-headed

- Feelings of unreality, or being disconnected from oneself

- Fear of losing control or going crazy

- Fear that rapidly builds to a peak within 10 minutes or less

- Fear of imminent danger or impending doom

- Urges to escape the situation in which the attack is occurring

- Going to emergency rooms and having medical evaluations for these physical symptoms

Panic attacks cause people to believe they're going to lose control, have a heart attack or stroke, or go crazy. The impact of these psychological and physical meltdowns increases the person's avoidance of particular contaminants and the things associated with the one that precipitated the attack. The washing rituals that follow severe attacks can continue nonstop, ending only because the person is physically exhausted. The sufferer's amazing capacity to endure torture inflicted by washing rituals, which are frequently injurious to the skin, is driven by the erroneous belief that the distress from them is not as bad as the possible catastrophes from failing to do them. As the disorder worsens, the person starts using washing rituals preventatively, when they're not anxious, or only mildly anxious. They see this as some kind of a psychological immunization against high anxiety and panic.

The main point here is that people who dread contamination use washing as a behavioral vaccination to prevent anxiety and panic attacks. But this is a false vaccine that is the equivalent of a placebo, a sugar pill. It does nothing; the anxiety will diminish anyway without ritualizing. And another irony is that the rituals start as a way of eliminating anxiety, but the more they're used, the more they themselves become sources of anxiety. As you can see, rituals are not only useless but actually harmful. You'll learn how to replace them with effective methods for eliminating washing compulsions and hypersensitivity to contamination in the following chapters.

Fear of Unending Skin Irritations

A fair number of people complain about the way their skin feels after contact with a contaminant. Some say it feels like there is a film covering the area of skin that was touched. Others say it's a persistent annoyance they can't label, and so distracting they can't block it out. All those with these reactions find the experience extremely aggravating and use washing to relieve it, believing that without doing so their distress would be unending.

Fear of Illness and Disease

The most common fear from contamination is of contracting illnesses or diseases that range from simply "not feeling well" to potentially fatal ailments. When I first started working with OCD patients, HIV and AIDS had just been discovered and concern about them was not as great as it is nowadays. Then, cancer was feared the most, but now it's AIDS and sexually transmitted diseases (STDs). However, when a person is not in the grip of an obsession, they can see that these fears are unrealistic, and the things they're avoiding are not truly harmful. But when they're bedeviled by obsessions, rationality is hijacked and anxiety reigns, which activates fleeing from the danger and doing rituals. Given that obsessional fears are irrational, the particular things avoided and rituals performed are rarely realistically related to the ailments they're intended to prevent. Practicing unreasonable behaviors such as not touching doorknobs or other things people touch, spending three to four hours in the shower, and hand washing thirty times a day prevent nothing but living a normal life.

Fear of Spreading Contamination

People who fear being contaminated may also worry about spreading their contamination to other people and objects. Of course, this makes their world even more restrictive, because as more and more things become contaminated, the more vigilant they must become to avoid them, and the more time and energy spent ritualizing after contact occurs.

▪ Grace's Story: Preserving Purity

Grace was an eighteen-year-old college student who lived with her parents and younger brother. She could tolerate feeling grimy while out in the world and attending classes, however on arriving home she had to decontaminate for about forty-five minutes through ritualized hand and arm washing. From then on, with the exception of being in her room, she avoided spreading contamination by keeping her hands at waist level with her palms up, like a surgeon who had just scrubbed and is keeping her hands sterile by not touching anything. When she needed to take hold of something she would use a tissue, her sleeves, or gloves. To avoid contaminating her hands and to keep from spreading contamination when they were dirty, Grace developed expertise in using her feet, elbows, forearms, and other body parts to open and close doors, turn on lights, slide chairs in and out to sit in, turn on faucets and the stove, flush toilets, and manipulate many other things. Her room was a pristine sanctuary in which neither people nor anything that hadn't been properly sanitized was permitted. Schoolbooks and other nonwashable materials needed for homework were used at the kitchen table, and when she was finished with them, placed in a backpack outside her room. A round of hand and arm washing would occur each time she reentered her safe place. Family members participated in her contamination prevention procedures, and when they inadvertently spoiled something, Grace would become almost hysterical and spend two to three hours showering until it felt right to stop. You can readily appreciate the extent to which her and her family's life revolved around avoidance, washing, and cleaning rituals.

Fear of Contaminating Others

Some people aren't concerned about becoming contaminated themselves but fear they can contaminate others, including family members. For instance, I worked with a young mother who could not have direct physical contact with her three-year-old son for fear of making him ill. Yet, this was not a problem with her husband or anyone else. She also "protected" the child from having contact with things she had touched. To prevent illness, the mother used gloves, tissues, and other ways of blocking skin-to-skin contact. When slip-ups happened, the child was undressed at once, bathed, and after that clad in clean clothes. The mother maintained elaborate procedures to keep the child's clothes, dishes, eating utensils, toys, and other belongings as isolated as possible from the rest of the household in order to avoid contamination. No one else was allowed to care for the little fellow because she couldn't trust them to maintain her high level of protection against contamination. Inevitably, this caused problems with her marriage, her parents, and in-laws. More importantly, the child's development was jeopardized. Realizing this, the mother used behavior therapy and medications to overcome her fears and rituals.

Fear of Unique Consequences

We have just reviewed the most common fears—threats to mental or physical health—that trigger compulsive washing. Yet washing is used as the ritual of choice to get relief triggered by circumstances having nothing to do with illness or disease. Recall the examples of the man who had to wash if he encountered things related to firefighters, the woman who had to shower when ideas of blindness occurred to her, and the man who washed his hands and kitchen to prevent suicide. These are but a few of the countless varieties of unique consequences that have been and will be dictated by OCD.

If your fears seem unique, don't worry about it. It doesn't mean that they are any more serious than the common ones of illness and disease. They may be singular, but only in the way they look, not in the way they work. Remember, regardless of the content of obsessions or type of rituals used to deal with them, OCD always works the same way in everyone. That is, irrational thoughts, images, and impulses repeatedly break into your consciousness and instantaneously trigger anxiety and the dread of the future. Try as you might, you cannot squelch the thoughts or images nor extinguish the distress. Somehow you learn that repeating certain washing behaviors, exhausting as they might be, eventually offers some relief, though temporary because the cycle is inevitably triggered again and again. It doesn't matter what the particular triggers, obsessions, or rituals are; they all operate in the same pattern to set off and maintain pathological emotions that are life-interfering. Unique or not, all symptoms follow this pattern during the course of the disorder, and more importantly as you shall see, all symptoms respond to treatment.

RITUALS TRIGGERED BY FEAR

The fear from obsessions trigger compulsions because they, for the time being, bring relief. As you gathered from the previous section, people frequently use washing to do this. This section will discuss the many ways that rituals are performed. Recall that repeated mental activities are also compulsions used to reduce distress. So they will be reviewed as well.

Avoidance Behaviors

The first safeguard against contamination is avoidance of contact with anything of questionable cleanliness. Avoidance behaviors range from those that are hardly noticeable, like touching certain objects with only one hand, to those that restrict a person to the confines of his or her home. And they often take place even there. Listed below are but a few of the common avoidance strategies:

- Staying away from things other people touch, such as doorknobs, doorbells, light switches, railings, handles, telephones, automatic tellers, money, water fountains, faucets, and toilet flushers

- Keeping people at a distance to prevent handshakes, hugs, kisses, sexual intimacy, exposure to sneezes, coughs, spittle, and so on

- Shunning certain people, even loved ones, and things they have touched because they feel contaminated

- Requiring family members to decontaminate before entering the home by removing clothes, washing, showering, or taking other decontamination actions

- Waiting for other people to open doors or press elevator buttons for floors

- Having others turn on water faucets, open refrigerators, operate TV remote controls, etc.

- Preventing other people from being in certain rooms, areas, or using particular items

- Throwing away serviceable clothes and items

- Trying on or wearing new clothes only after they have been washed

- Never taking the top item in a stack or an item from the front row on a shelf in a market

- Not touching or picking up things that fall on the ground or are close to it, such as shoes, shoelaces, cuffs, or pant legs

- Pulling sleeves of shirts, sweaters, and jackets over hands to touch doorknobs, telephones, and other objects people use

- Using tissues, disposable gloves, or plastic bags to grasp items

- Using hand wipes or disinfectant sprays for cleaning items before touching them

- Using feet, legs, elbows, wrists, shoulders, rear end, and other body parts to open doors, move furniture, and other things

- Severely restricting food and liquid intake and delaying elimination as long as possible to minimize contact with bodily waste

- Using toilets outside the home by covering the seats with multiple sheets of paper or without sitting on them

- Undressing completely to have bowel movements so clothing isn't contaminated

- Using laxatives and suppositories to completely evacuate bowels

- Sitting on the toilet for hours to be certain bowels are completely empty

- Making excuses to skirt medical and dental examinations, doctors' offices, hospitals, and other necessary health-care professionals and facilities

Washing and Cleaning Rituals

Practicing avoidance activities, as most of you know, requires constant vigilance to spot danger and avoid it when you can. When you can't, you suffer distress until you engage in the rituals. Moreover, even on the best of days there is no certainty that you have completely evaded contamination. So compulsions, despite your earnest intentions to limit or prevent them, happen. Here's a short list of common ones.

Washing

When feeling contaminated, people do the following:

- Use personal bars of soap, hand wipes, pocket-sized hand gels, alcohol, antiseptic solutions, disinfectants, or bleaches to clean the "contaminated" body parts or objects

- Use excessive amounts of soap, frequently the liquid kind that is dispensed from a bottle, which they buy by the case thinking more soap will make them "cleaner"

- Repeatedly soap and rinse their hands and arms for an hour or more at a time

- Wash their hands twenty to thirty or more times per day causing bleeding and skin lesions

- Use face cloths and towels only one time

- Shower each time they return home, as many as four to five times per day

- Shower for an hour or more at a time, and in severe cases, up to five hours or more

- Shower or bathe using scalding water and abrasive cleaning utensils such as granulated soaps, pumice stones, scrub brushes, and even sandpaper

- Wash and shower while using mental rituals like counting, saying nonsense words, having positive thoughts and images in order to neutralize distressing ones

- Always wash body parts in the same order to prevent something "bad" from happening

- Schedule urination and bowel movements only immediately before showering

- Wipe excessively after bowel movements, causing bleeding and stopped-up toilets

- Compulsively seek medical consultation, contact prominent researchers, and do research on the illness or disease that frightens them by using libraries and the Internet

Cleaning

Many sufferers fear the spread of contamination, which activates excessive cleaning activities in an ongoing war against it. They can:

- Vacuum and scrub floors, countertops, and surfaces for hours on a daily basis

- Replace difficult to clean surfaces with ones easier to wash (like replacing wall-to-wall carpeting with tile)

- Ruin nonwashable items by washing them

- Designate certain clothing items as contaminated that are laundered separately and specially

- Use elaborate cleaning procedures to purify the washer and dryer after doing laundry

- Unnecessarily sterilize and disinfect items to the extent of damaging them

Reassurance

A very common ritual, triggered by all types of obsessions, is reassurance seeking. People with washing and cleaning compulsions will repeatedly ask friends and family to assure them that their fears are unrealistic; that they will not be visited by illness, disease, or other threats posed by their OCD demon. When told what they want to hear, the person may be comforted, but only for the short term. Invariably, the old fears return and new ones occur, and the reassurance requests continue, indefinitely, until stopped by techniques you'll learn in chapter 8.

False Fear Blockers—Real Health Hazards

Contrary to the intentions of people who use them, the above rituals have no realistic effect on alleviating their unrealistic fears. However, they can have damaging effects on their health. The fear of germs associated with doctors, dentists, emergency rooms, and hospitals causes the avoidance of routine medical and dental examinations necessary for illness and disease prevention, as well as the treatment of acute and chronic illnesses. Holding urine and feces leads to urinary tract and gastrointestinal problems. Washing rituals using caustic skin cleansers and abrasive scouring cause lesions that become infected. And excessive tooth brushing and flossing result in gum disease.

Summary

The rituals you have developed blunt your distress for a short time, but the triggers for obsessions are everywhere and unavoidable, and the cycle restarts. This you know from your experience. Though the washing and cleaning compulsions are false fear-blockers, they're all you have to rely on for now. This will change, because you're going to learn effective strategies for dismantling and putting to rest this contamination-washing cycle.

In this chapter, we reviewed the way the contamination-washing cycle operates, some of the common obsessions you may have developed, and some typical rituals created due to these obsessions. In the next chapter, we'll start disrupting the contamination-washing cycle by taking inventories of the triggers for your particular obsessive fears and your rituals for responding to them.

CHAPTER 3

Self-Assessment

Although this book focuses exclusively on overcoming washing compulsions, it is important to identify any additional OCD symptoms you may have. Many people with OCD have more than one subtype of the disorder. For instance, a person can have washing compulsions and checking compulsions. By completing the checklists that follow, you'll know if you have more symptoms than compulsive washing. If so, consider consultation with a mental-health professional. Or, if you wish to use a self-help method, books are available that address OCD subtypes that are not discussed here. You'll find them in the Resources section of this book. It is important to complete the following self-assessments:

- Survey of Obsessions and Compulsions for OCD (SOC-OCD)

- Distress and Interference from OCD (DI-OCD)

SURVEY OF OBSESSIONS AND COMPULSIONS FOR OBSESSIVE-COMPULSIVE DISORDER (SOC-OCD)

The purpose of this checklist is to identify your obsessions and compulsions and assess their severity. This will enable you to pinpoint your specific symptoms and eliminate or significantly decrease them.

Obsessions

Obsessions are unwelcome and distressing thoughts, images, or impulses that repeatedly occur. They may seem to happen against your will, and seem to get stuck in your mind. They may be repugnant, even though you may know they are senseless and don't fit your personality. An example of an obsession is the recurrent thought or impulse to physically harm someone even though you know you never would.

The word "fear" is frequently used for the word "obsession," because the obsession activates fear almost instantaneously, making the two events feel like they are happening as one. The word "worry" is also used for "obsessions"; for example, when some people with OCD talk of "worries" they are having, they are really talking about obsessions. Perhaps more commonly, obsessions are simply referred to as "thoughts," even when they are actually in the form of images or impulses. These terms will be used interchangeably throughout the checklist.

Contamination Obsessions

These obsessions revolve around contact with things that cause fears of being unclean, feeling disgusted, becoming ill or diseased, or having endless anxiety and/or nervous breakdowns. Check any of the items below that cause you an excessive amount of worry.

☐   Bodily substances (for example, blood, urine, feces, saliva, perspiration, or semen)

☐   Germs

☐   Dirt or filth

☐   Greasy, sticky items

☐   Environmental contaminants (for example, garbage, litter, radiation, mercury, lead, toxic waste, batteries, or microwave ovens)

☐   Household contaminants (for example, insecticides, household cleansers, solvents, or glass cleaners)

☐   Things other people touch

☐   Animals or insects

☐   Medications

☐   Illness or disease from contamination (for example, AIDS, cancer, tuberculosis, etc.)

☐   Spreading contamination and causing illness to others

☐   High contamination anxiety that may not end and/or that might cause a nervous breakdown

☐   Other sources of contamination. Write a brief description.

_____

_____

Obsessions of Being Irresponsible or Careless

These are obsessions about making mistakes, not paying attention to what you're doing, and/or being careless or irresponsible. Check all that apply.

☐   Fear of causing harm because you are careless and irresponsible (for example, leaving the stove or other appliances on or being reckless or inattentive)

☐   Fear of running over someone without knowing it

☐   Fear of handwriting or other actions not being perfect

☐   Fear of communicating incorrect information

☐   Fear of being blamed or criticized for frequent mistakes

☐   Fear you'll accidentally reveal something about yourself you don't want others to know

☐   Other fears about being careless or irresponsible. Write a brief description.

_____

_____

Harm Obsessions

These are worries about harming yourself or others. Check all that apply.

☐   Fear of harming yourself (for example, by stabbing yourself or driving into oncoming traffic)

☐   Fear of harming others (for example, beating, stabbing, or poisoning someone)

☐   Repeated violent or horrific images in your head (for example, scenes of killing family members or of mutilated bodies)

☐   Fear of blurting out unacceptable statements in public (for example, obscenities or insults)

☐   Fear of doing something embarrassing (for example, taking your clothes off in public or kissing strangers)

☐   Fear of acting on unwanted harmful impulses (for example, sticking your finger in a running electric fan or setting off fire alarms)

☐   Fear from other obsessions involving harm. Write a brief description.

_____

_____

Sexual Obsessions

These obsessions revolve around unwanted sexual thoughts, images, or impulses. Check all that apply.

☐   Having sex with family members

☐   Having sex with children

☐   Having sex with animals

☐   Engaging in sexual activities that are incompatible with your sexual orientation

☐   Committing aggressive sexual acts against others

☐   Other unwanted sexual thoughts, images, or urges. Write a brief description.

_____

_____

Religious/Scrupulosity Obsessions

The main fear here is of being dishonest, sinful, or evil. Check all that apply.

☐   Fear of committing blasphemy by showing contempt for or irreverence to God

☐   Fear of sacrilegious thoughts (for example, violating religious beliefs)

☐   Fear of being possessed

☐   Excessive concern with right and wrong and about being honest

☐   Fear of cheating someone

☐   Fear of telling lies

☐   Fear of having other anti-religious thoughts or committing other dishonest acts. Write a brief description.

_____

_____

Saving and Collecting Obsessions: Hoarding

Accumulating possessions that are rarely used or discarded is irresistible for those with this obsession. Check all that apply.

- ☐ Fear of making a mistake by throwing away something that may be valuable or useful

- ☐ Difficulty throwing away seemingly useless items

- ☐ Irresistible urges to collect and save useless items (for example, newspapers, junk mail, food wrappers and containers, old clothes, or items others have discarded)

- ☐ Other hoarding obsessions. Write a brief description.

_____

_____

Obsessions about Symmetry or Exactness

This obsession causes those with it to be anxious until items and objects are arranged perfectly or symmetrically. Check all that apply.

- ☐ Noticing things that are out of order

- ☐ Noticing things that are not as they should be

- ☐ Other obsessions about symmetry or exactness. Write a brief description.

_____

_____

Somatic Obsessions

These obsessions involve repeated checking of physical symptoms or aspects of one's body or appearance. Check all that apply.

- ☐ Excessive concern about illness or disease (for example, almost continuous worry about major illnesses despite the lack of medical evidence)

☐ Excessive worry about some aspect of your appearance (for example, facial features, hair, or body shape)

☐ Other somatic obsessions not listed. Write a brief description.

_____

_____

Obsessions about Character Defects

At some point during the disorder, it seems that most people worry that the OCD means something about them as a person—about their moral fiber. They may even believe that they don't have OCD and that their obsessions are actually an expression of their true nature. They believe that because these are their thoughts, they must *want* to think them or carry them out. No matter how hard others try to convince them that this is a misconception, they persist in this belief. These distorted self-perceptions are secondary obsessions about the meaning of the primary obsessions. Please be assured that they are simply another aspect of the disorder and vanish with the elimination of the primary obsessions. Check off all the thoughts you have about yourself.

☐ Your symptoms are caused by a major character defect.

☐ You're crazy.

☐ You'll lose control.

☐ You're not good enough.

☐ You're basically stained.

☐ You're irresponsible or careless.

☐ You're a killer.

☐ You're a sexual deviant.

☐ You're a sinner.

☐   You're a bad person.

☐   You have some other personality defect not listed. Write a brief description.

_____

_____

Miscellaneous Obsessions

These obsessions are like superstitions. Check all that apply.

☐   Fear of saying, hearing, or seeing certain words

☐   Fear of saying, hearing, or seeing certain numbers

☐   Fear of certain colors

☐   Other miscellaneous obsessions. Write a brief description.

_____

_____

Unique Obsessions

This category is for obsessions that are not listed above. They include any thoughts, images, or impulses that are unwanted, repetitive, persistent, and about the occurrence of highly unlikely or impossible events. Write a brief description.

_____

_____

_____

_____

_____

Compulsions

Compulsions are behaviors or mental activities that you perform to reduce distress even though you may know these rituals are senseless or excessive. At times, you may try to resist doing them, but this may prove difficult, especially when the anxiety doesn't stop until the compulsion is completed. An example of a compulsion is the need to repeatedly wash your hands, "decontaminate" your clothes or other objects, or shower for long periods of time to make sure you are clean.

Most compulsions are observable behaviors, but some are unobservable mental activities, such as silent checking; having to recite nonsense phrases to yourself each time you have a bad thought; repeating special words, numbers, or images; saying prayers, lucky numbers, or counting; reliving past events; or going over conversations that occurred. They can also be of a more intellectual nature, such as going over reasons why the fears won't materialize.

Washing Compulsions

These compulsions are used to relieve fears of being contaminated. Check all that apply.

- ☐ Wash hands excessively and/or in a ritualized way

- ☐ Shower, bathe, brush teeth, floss, groom, or do toilet routines in a ritualized and/or excessive way

- ☐ Excessively clean household objects or other things people touch

- ☐ Use other steps to prevent or remove contamination

- ☐ Engage in other repetitive actions or thoughts involving contamination fears. Write a brief description.

_____

_____

Checking Compulsions

These compulsions are used to alleviate fears of being irresponsible or careless. Check all that apply.

- ☐ Checking locks, stoves, appliances, or vehicles

- ☐ Checking that you didn't run over someone

- ☐ Checking what you write

- ☐ Mentally reviewing conversations with other people

- ☐ Checking yourself (for example, checking to make sure your hygiene, grooming and appearance are just right)

- ☐ Checking that others are safe

- ☐ Checking that some dreaded harm did not or will not happen

- ☐ Checking that you did not accidentally reveal something about yourself that you don't want others to know

- ☐ Engaging in any other checking behaviors. Write a brief description.

_____

_____

Repeating Compulsions

To prevent something bad from happening or to feel better, do you use any of the following compulsions? Check all that apply.

- ☐ Repeating various actions or behaviors (for example, putting clothes on and taking them off, turning lights on and off, or retracing your steps when walking or your route when driving)

- ☐ Rereading or rewriting

☐ Making certain movements, gestures, or verbalizations to relieve distress

☐ Confessing excessively, making unnecessary self-disclosures

☐ Other forms of repeating not listed. Write a brief description.

_____

_____

Mental Compulsions

Compulsions of this sort take place in your head. To relieve distress, the person thinks certain thoughts or creates mental images immediately following the obsession. Frequently, these mental rituals are in response to obsessions about violence, sex, and religion. Check all that apply.

☐ Visualizing a good image to nullify a bad image

☐ Trying to have a good thought to neutralize a bad thought

☐ Having to repeat a behavior you were doing when a bad thought happens until you have a good thought

☐ Using counting or spelling to offset an obsession

☐ Silently reciting prayers or certain words or phrases

☐ Talking out loud to yourself, or saying, "No, no, no, no . . ." repeatedly in an attempt to undo thoughts, impulses, or images

☐ Going over lists of reasons why your fears are unfounded

☐ Sitting down and "thinking things through" to prove to yourself that you have nothing to fear

☐ Trying to challenge the reality of your fears

☐   Saying to yourself, "It's not me, it's OCD."

☐   Mentally reviewing past events to be sure they happened the way you wanted them to

☐   Mentally replaying conversations

☐   Seeking information about your fear by reading, using the Internet, asking experts, etc.

☐   Using other means of rationalizing your fears

☐   Using any other mental rituals to "protect" yourself. Write a brief description.

_____

_____

Hoarding and/or Collecting Compulsions

These compulsions are attempts to satisfy insatiable drives to collect things, or avoid the fear of throwing away something that might be important or could be useful later. Check all that apply.

☐   Rarely discarding anything

☐   Collecting large amounts of stuff that other people regard as junk

☐   Renting storage space for collected items

☐   Filling living space with unused clutter

☐   Other hoarding and/or collecting compulsions not listed. Write a brief description.

_____

_____

Symmetry and/or Exactness Compulsions

People with these compulsions are trying to meet the demands imposed by obsessions about symmetry and/or exactness. Check all that apply.

- ☐ Arranging clothes in closets, books on shelves, objects on tables, and so forth, according to certain rules

- ☐ Avoiding having people in your home because they will disturb things

- ☐ Avoiding using appliances, books, CDs, or going into areas in your home because it's too much trouble to restore them to their original condition

- ☐ Any other types of compulsions related to symmetry and/or exactness. Write a brief description.

_____

_____

Somatic Compulsions

These compulsions are used to reduce fears from excessive worry about illness, disease, or some concern about your appearance. Check all that apply.

- ☐ Repeatedly examining yourself (for example, feeling for cancerous lumps, taking blood pressure, pulse, or temperature)

- ☐ Constantly looking at yourself in the mirror checking on certain aspects of your appearance

- ☐ Trying to cover up or hide what you consider to be defects in your appearance

- ☐ Other types of somatic compulsions. Write a brief description.

_____

_____

Miscellaneous Compulsions

The following are other common compulsions that people develop. Check all that apply.

☐   Writing lists excessively

☐   Engaging in superstitious behaviors

☐   Touching, tapping, or rubbing things

☐   Other miscellaneous compulsions. Write a brief description.

_____

_____

Unique Compulsions

There are unique compulsions, just as there are unique obsessions. If you engage in any behavioral or mental rituals that are not listed above, please write a brief description of them.

_____

_____

Additional Fears and Coping Attempts

People with OCD mainly bank on rituals to decrease distress from obsessions, but they also try additional ways to get relief. The following checklist can help you identify any use of faulty coping strategies.

Distraction

Probably the most common way, at least in the beginning, of dealing with obsessions is to focus your attention on something else. Please check all of the distraction techniques that apply.

☐   Paying extra attention to what you're doing

☐   Deliberately worrying about real-life problems

☐   Concentrating on work, chores, or some other activity

☐   Always keeping busy to keep obsessions off your mind

☐   Using other ways of distracting yourself. Write a brief description.

_____

_____

Avoidance

People with OCD try to prevent fear by avoiding certain circumstances. Check all that apply.

☐   Specific people

☐   Certain types of people

☐   Certain activities

☐   Certain TV programs, news reports, or movies

☐   Particular objects

☐   Certain places

☐   Other situations. Write a brief description.

_____

_____

Reassurance

People with OCD frequently ask others to reassure them that their fears will not come true. Please check any of the following ways that you ask for reassurance.

☐   Getting people to tell you your fears will not happen

☐   Asking others about various aspects of your fears

☐   Managing to get others to say things that relieve your fear

☐   Any other means to get reassurance. Write a brief description.

_____

_____

UNDERSTANDING THE RESULTS OF THE SOC-OCD

If you checked any of the items below, it suggests that you have OCD that manifests itself in the form of irrational fears of being contaminated or dirtied by objects or situations that pose no real threat. These obsessions likely cause you to compulsively wash.

- Bodily substances (for example, blood, urine, feces, saliva, perspiration, or semen)

- Germs

- Dirt or filth

- Greasy, sticky items

- Environmental contaminants (for example, garbage, litter, radiation, mercury, lead, toxic waste, batteries, or microwave ovens)

- Household contaminants (for example, insecticides, household cleansers, solvents, or glass cleaners)

- Things other people touch

- Animals or insects

- Medications

- Illness or disease from contamination (for example, AIDS, cancer, tuberculosis, etc.)

- Spreading contamination and causing illness to others

- High contamination anxiety that may not end and/or that might cause a nervous breakdown

- Other sources of contamination

If you checked any other items, it is possible that you have additional subtypes of OCD as well. If you have obsessions and compulsions that are not listed above, and you are concerned about them, know that many people have unique symptoms which are as treatable as the common ones. As previously mentioned, consultation with a mental-health professional is advised. You can also learn more about other forms of OCD by referring to readings that are listed in the Resources section of this book.

DISTRESS AND INTERFERENCE FROM OCD (DI-OCD)

With the information you have from the above checklists, you know what your symptoms are. By completing the DI-OCD, you'll get an estimate of the severity of your symptoms and how much OCD interferes with your daily life. Do this by circling the number in the boxes below for each item that best indicates your feelings.

Part I: Distress from Symptoms	Not at all	A Little	Pretty Much	Very Much	Couldn't Be Worse
Obsessions	0	1	2	3	4
Compulsions	0	1	2	3	4
Avoidance	0	1	2	3	4
Low mood	0	1	2	3	4
Total Score: Add numbers circled above					

Part II: Interference with Daily Life	Not at all	A Little	Pretty Much	Very Much	Couldn't Be Worse
School, work, or usual routines	0	1	2	3	4
Social activities	0	1	2	3	4
Family relationships	0	1	2	3	4
Pleasurable activities	0	1	2	3	4
Total Score: Add numbers circled above					

Scoring and Interpreting Your Results

Add the numbers you circled in Part I and Part II separately. The table below shows where your score is in terms of your level of distress from symptoms and the amount OCD interferes with your daily life. Circle your distress levels from symptoms and interference with daily life.

Distress and Interference from OCD Scores	
Part I: **Distress from Symptoms Score**	**Level of Distress**
0–3	Normal
4–7	Mild
8–11	Moderate
12–16	Severe
Part II: **Interference with Daily Life Score**	**Level of Interference**
0–3	Normal
4–7	Mild
8–11	Moderate
12–16	Severe

For those with scores in the normal and mild ranges of severity, you can probably gain control of your symptoms through this book without the assistance of professional help. For those with scores in the moderate range, you may be able to gain control with this book. If after exerting sufficient effort you feel that your results are not satisfactory, I suggest you seek treatment from a behavior therapist. For those with scores in the severe range, using this book will probably not produce the results you desire. Therefore, I definitely recommend you seek treatment from a behavior therapist.

Summary

In this chapter, you had the opportunity to assess the severity of your condition. In the next chapter, you will begin your first treatment exercises. These will give you proof that by changing your behavior, you can reduce or eliminate your symptoms.

CHAPTER 4

Face, Embrace, and Erase the Fear

You have been using compulsions, reasoning, denial, avoidance, and distraction in an attempt to rid yourself of obsessions and have found these efforts futile. It is obvious that what you've been doing isn't working. Yet you persist with these activities because they offer a brief respite from distress—this lasting only until the onslaught of the next obsession. You have been practicing false fear-blocking behaviors that prevent recovery and maintain and strengthen symptoms. In this chapter, I'll introduce you to a method that does work, a form of exposure therapy that I call exposure, ritual prevention, and awareness therapy (ERPA). It essentially involves facing the fear, which is absolutely necessary for recovery. We will start by explaining the reasoning behind ERPA. Then, each of its components will be described and brought to life by a case example. In the next chapter, I'll guide you through developing your own treatment plan based on this information.

TREATMENT: THE IRONY OF DOING THE OPPOSITE

I remember a movie in which one of the characters went around asking people to define the word "irony." Although most of them seemed to know what it meant, they were unable to put it into words. It wasn't until the end of the movie that one of them gave a suitable definition. I'm reminded of this because the continuation and elimination of OCD symptoms are perfect examples of irony: the occurrence of outcomes that are the opposite of those that were intended. You have probably been steering clear of triggers for your obsessions and engaging in compulsions after contact with those you couldn't avoid. Ironically, instead of reducing your distress, what you have been doing is sustaining or even worsening your condition. To get out of this quagmire, you have to start doing the opposite of what you have been doing up until now. This means deliberately making contact with your triggers while refraining from your resulting compulsions. With enough exposure to your triggers, over a sufficient period of time, you will notice that they become powerless to provoke distress, and the absence of distress eliminates the need for compulsions. See what I mean about OCD and irony? Exposure, ritual prevention, and awareness exercises are used to achieve this.

EXPOSURE, RITUAL PREVENTION, AND AWARENESS EXERCISES

It is important that you understand how ERPA exercises are related to the way your symptoms work. So let's review the series of events that take place during a cycle of OCD symptoms, commonly called an OCD spike. First, there's a trigger, something you notice in your physical or mental world. Second, this trigger instantly activates an obsession—thoughts, feelings, or impulses that are distressful. Almost simultaneously, you feel fear, guilt, apprehension, dread, anger, or any number and combination of distressing emotions. These three events—exposure to a trigger, activation of an obsession, and feelings of distress—feel like they happen together, as a single event. Therefore, the terms, "trigger," "obsession," and "distress" are used interchangeably to refer to this seemingly single event—the OCD spike. Your natural reaction is to turn it off as quickly as possible. Consequently, by trial and error, you find out that by repeating certain actions and/or mental gyrations, you get temporary relief until the next obsession causes the same cycle to occur.

ERPA exercises address each event in the OCD spike. First, you select a trigger for a particular obsession-compulsion combination and then practice exposure to this trigger. During the exposure, you refrain from rituals and instead practice awareness of the distress. When this is done successfully, the distress fades away. Because the obsession that used to cause terrible anxiety no longer has that power, it becomes insignificant, making it intrusive and repetitive no more. In the absence of obsessions, there is no need for compulsions. The exercises have changed the brain, which in turn changes behaviors and emotions. Desensitization has occurred. The exposure exercise is the vehicle, the Rolls Royce of treatments, which delivers this result.

By practicing the exercises from one to one and a half hours per day (including weekends and holidays), you should make good progress. When this schedule is adhered to, most people desensitize themselves to the particular trigger they're working on within five to seven days. This success gives them a big dose of confidence that they can control their anxiety, and increases their motivation to pursue and eradicate it. They now truly believe they will become "scared fearless."

To put together an exposure exercise, you'll need to follow these steps:

1. Select an obsession-compulsion combination for elimination.

2. Practice exposure by bringing on the obsession in reality and in imagination.

3. Practice ritual prevention by refraining from engaging in compulsions and fear-blocking behaviors.

4. Practice awareness by fully experiencing the triggered thoughts, images, impulses, and feelings they set off.

I'll explain each of the above activities and illustrate them with examples from Betty's treatment.

SELECTING AN OBSESSION-COMPULSION COMBINATION FOR ELIMINATION

The first step is usually to target the obsession-compulsion combination that is least distressful. Even though you may be eager to get rid of the most troublesome of your symptoms, it's best to start with the one that you will have the greatest chance of success in overcoming. After all, nothing succeeds like success. Don't worry; we will eventually deal with all of your triggers. As you're aware, there will be some stress associated with the exercises you are about to undertake. So start with the easiest one first to keep the distress at a minimum.

Subjective Units of Distress Scale

At this point I'd like to introduce the Subjective Units of Distress Scale (SUDS) used for estimating the amount of distress you feel from obsessions. Using numbers makes it easier to compare the strength of different triggers and to measure our success in eliminating them. Think of the worst OCD spike that you've ever had and how it felt. Give this a SUDS level of 100. Now think of how it feels to be in a deep state of relaxation and give this a SUDS level of 0 (see figure 2).

| 0 | 10 | 20 | 30 | 40 | 50 | 60 | 70 | 80 | 90 | 100 |
| Mild | | | | | Moderate | | | | | Severe |

Figure 2: Subjective Units of Distress Scale (SUDS)

Use this scale to keep track of the changes in your distress from the exposure exercises. For example, a particular trigger might initially cause a SUDS level of 10 to 20, and after several exposure exercises, it could go down to 5 to 7. In selecting triggers for elimination, it's best to start with those with a SUDS level of about 20 to 30.

■ Betty's Story: Measuring SUDS

Let's use Betty as an example of how to use SUDS levels for choosing a treatment target. The first obsession-compulsion combination she chose to go after was her fear of a couch and chair in her home that she felt were contaminated, and her compulsion to wash after touching them. She gave this obsession-compulsion combination a SUDS level of 20.

EXPOSURE: BRINGING ON THE OBSESSIONS

Exposure involves making contact with triggers for your obsessions in reality, in the outer, physical and social world, or in imaginary situations, which are in the inner, mental world. Both types basically work the same way, because fear is the problem and fear is the solution. I realize that the idea of facing fear is quite scary, but it's necessary. In case after case, patients have reported that once they start confronting fear, they find it not nearly as distressful as anticipated. More importantly, they discover that exposure works. The obsessions stop triggering fear and just become "thoughts." Being neutral with no emotional impact, they are insignificant and gradually fade away.

Shaping

Keep in mind that the exposure exercises are done in a gradual way, moving toward a goal slowly. This gradual way of making progress is called *shaping*. Start with a situation that causes only minimal distress and stay with it until you have little or no reaction to it. Only then do you move on to another situation, one that's only slightly more difficult than the first one. You then stick with that one until the distress evaporates. This process is continued until you have been thoroughly exposed to all of your obsessions, including the ones you initially estimated to be the most frightening. By the time you get to more difficult fears, you will have been desensitized by the exposure exercises leading up to them, so that the final step will be no more difficult than the first one. Moving toward a goal in small steps is an important part of the recovery process. I explain this to our patients by telling them the following fable, which is based on an actual case.

■ The Lady Who Learned to Love Rats

Once upon a time, there was a lady who had OCD in the form of a fear of contamination from rats. She feared they were everywhere and had contaminated everything. She became almost homebound. On coming home from the rare occasions that she did go out, she washed compulsively to prevent illness or death. After years of ineffective treatments, she learned about exposure therapy. After months of searching for a therapist skilled in the technique, she found one. After weeks of putting off an appointment, she scheduled one. Here's what happened.

The therapist had her stand at the one-yard line of a football field and simply look at a rat, one hundred yards away at the other end of the field. She felt mildly fearful and wanted to look away, but responded to encouragement to continue gazing upon the rat while noticing the fear. She was asked to rate her fear on a scale from 0 to 100, with 0 being absolutely no fear and 100 being the most distress she ever had from OCD. At first her fear rating was between 20 and 30. However, after standing at the one-yard line watching the rat for a while, she felt it go down and then it went away completely.

The next step was to move toward the rat, just a few yards, enough to raise her fear level up to 20 or 30 again. She remained at that spot, continuing to look at the rodent as she had before, until her fear dropped to 0. With each step her brain's fear system was learning that nothing dangerous was happening. The rat was not attacking her, and the fear was diminishing of its own accord, without avoidance or any mental or physical rituals. All she had to do was pay attention to her fear and its decline. The confidence that came from her dropping fear emboldened her to keep on moving toward her goal. She continued her courageous trek until she was only one yard from the rat. Then she stood right in front of it, and finally, at what was once the peak of her fear mountain, she picked it up, caressed it, and said, "You're so cute."

I hope this fable helps you follow through with the treatment. At this point, not knowing what to expect, your fear and apprehension of exposure therapy are at their highest, probably even greater than the fear you will in fact experience. In real life, arranging shaping is not as easy as in the fable, but you can take as much time as you need because *you* set the pace. Find your own gridiron and shape your way out of OCD.

Prolonged Exposure

For exposure to succeed in erasing your fear, there are two necessary conditions. First, rituals, and any other means of dodging the exposure, must be prevented. The use of false fear-blockers will be fully discussed in the next section. For now, let's discuss the second of these conditions: prolonged, repeated exposures. These must be long enough for you to experience a noticeable decline in your distress during the course of the session. This means having direct contact with contaminants for as long as it takes to notice a decrease in your distress. This could be for as long as an hour. What people typically feel during their sessions is a gradual rise in distress, which levels off after several minutes. Then it starts to decline. It is during this phase that you're receiving the benefits of the exercise. Whatever the trigger, it's losing its power to provoke fear. With the next exposure session, and subsequent ones, you'll find that the fear at the beginning is lower and falls away faster, until, eventually, you'll feel little or no distress at all. You will have neutralized the trigger, and learned that exposure alone will free you from anxiety without resorting to the use of false fear-blockers. (See figure 3, a graph depicting the rise and fall of distress over time.)

Keep your exposure sessions to no more than ninety minutes by selecting triggers that are in the mild to moderate range of difficulty. Exposure can be mentally and emotionally draining, so you don't want to cause yourself unnecessary hardship by overdoing it. If you underestimate the power of a trigger and find that it's

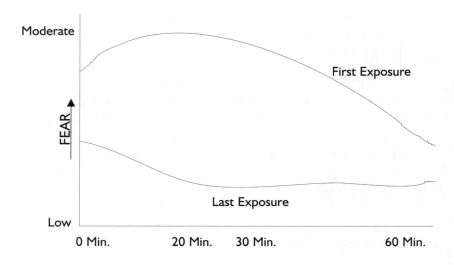

Figure 3: Getting Used to It

taking more than ninety minutes for the distress to decrease, stop working on it and replace it with an easier exercise. You can return to the one you underestimated after the easier exercises have desensitized you.

As mentioned above, exposure exercises can be done in reality or in your imagination. Exposures in reality aim to eliminate obsessions triggered by situations in the real world, your physical and social environment. Exposure activities of this kind require being physically involved with situations that trigger obsessions. Exposures in imagination aim to eliminate obsessions triggered by thoughts and images of imagined dreaded future events that are impossible or improbable. Exposures of this kind require contact with the imagined triggers since these triggers exist only in your mind. This is done quite effectively with audiotape exposures (listening to tape recorded scenarios about the feared thoughts or images). Imaginal exposure is also used when exposure in reality is not possible because the trigger cannot actually be confronted, for example, fearing that you will develop HIV because you touched a doorknob. There will be more on this later in the book.

For either type of exposure exercise, it is of the utmost impor-
tance that you do not stop the exposure while your anxiety is up. If
you do, desensitization is prevented, and you can even be *sensitized*
further to the situation you're trying to neutralize. With this in mind,
schedule your exposure sessions when you have enough time to complete them and know that you will not be interrupted or distracted.
The best results are obtained when you practice every day, including
weekends and holidays. A momentum develops that makes the practice easier, causing faster results. I also recommend that you do the
exercises early in the day. This way you're less likely to put them off
and the thought of doing them is not hanging over your head like the
sword of Damocles for the bulk of the day.

■ Betty's Story: Exposure

Let's make of use Betty's treatment experience as an example, starting with exposure exercises she did in reality. As
you may recall, she chose making contact with a couch
and chair she feared to be contaminated in her home as
her first assignment. Before starting the exercises, she
avoided even being in the area where the furniture was.
Betty had been practicing these avoidance behaviors for
many months and had completely forgotten how the couch
and chair became contaminated, but staying away from
them had become automatic, as it had with other tainted
items in the house. She couldn't remember when she last
sat on either piece of furniture or how it affected her,
which was the reason she picked them to start with.

Her first exercise was to practice exposure to the
chair, the easier of the two she thought, in a gradual way
by lightly placing her outstretched hand on it for about
half an hour. Betty knew she was not to wash her hands
after this contact. Instead, she was to pay attention to the
distressing thoughts and physical sensations they triggered.
While her hand was on the chair and the distress was ris-
ing, she rationalized that she could wash her hand if she
wanted to, regardless of the dictates of therapy. But she
brushed this cop-out aside and refocused on the distressing

sensations in her palm and fingers, her increasing heart and respiration rates, and the perspiration on her forehead. After about thirty minutes she felt some relief and removed her hand. It was a little clammy, but the worst part was over; she had done it and it hadn't been as bad as she had anticipated.

Betty's next step was to touch many household objects in order to spread the contamination as an act of defying OCD and desensitizing herself to its irrational fears, all the while, resisting sporadic urges to wash or clean. She practiced touching the chair daily, with decreasing urges to wash, and after a few days she could touch it with both hands and spread the contamination with no anxiety.

Actually, she found the exercise easier than she had expected. This frequently happens when a person has been avoiding something for a long time. When they eventually have contact with it, they're surprised that it no longer alarms them. Over time, their conditioned fear response has extinguished. So in choosing your first exposure exercises, consider those situations, objects, or circumstances with the longest history of avoidance. Betty may have had some intuitive sense of this phenomenon that prompted her choosing the chair to work on first. Nevertheless, her first choice was the right choice because the exercise worked. She did have reservations, though, about the consequences of touching things around the house with her contaminated hands. For the most part she had tried to use them normally, but she did fudge on touching some things that triggered dreaded thoughts and images about HIV or some other STD. To address these imagined future catastrophes, she did exposure in her imagination with the aid of audiotaped scenarios. We wrote the following scenario, which I recorded for her to listen to.

For the first time in a long time you have deliberately spread contamination about the house. You know that it is part of an exercise to eliminate your fear of contamination and washing and cleaning compulsions. But this knowledge isn't helping to stop the anxiety and physical sensations that go with it that you now feel. You touched many things, some of which you can't remember, and they are now contaminated. You know this doesn't make sense, but the anxious feelings you're having are not reassuring. It's just the opposite. You're believing that you should have been more cautious and not spread the contamination to the extent that you did. But it's too late now, you've done it, and these actions mean that your worst fears could come true. At some time in the future you might have to grapple with the possibility of HIV or some other sexually transmitted disease. It's too late to do any washing and cleaning now. It won't do any good because you can't undo what's been done. You'll just have to suffer this distress, not knowing if or when it could be over.

Betty listened to the tape over and over again every day for about an hour and a half, each time, to begin with. She noticed during the first session that her anxiety started at a SUDS level of about 60 and dropped to about 40 after listening to the tape. After listening for a week, the scenario only provoked anxiety at a SUDS level of 10 or less. The thoughts it stimulated were losing their punch and even started seeming ridiculous. This is a common example of the benefits that come from changing behavior by approaching feared situations instead of avoiding them. Exposure exercises change emotions from high anxiety to low anxiety, and allow rational thoughts to replace irrational ones. When Betty moved on to the next exposure activity, the couch, she approached it with some confidence, in contrast to the trepidation she had about working on the chair.

RITUAL PREVENTION: REFRAINING FROM FALSE FEAR-BLOCKING BEHAVIOR

A false fear-blocker is any action or thought immediately following an obsession that reduces the fear. I use the term "false" because the reduced fear is only temporary and always returns with the next obsession. Their greatest harm is blocking exposure, which prevents recovery.

The most common false fear-blockers are:

- Physical and mental compulsions

- Distraction

- Avoidance

- Reasoning

- Reassurance seeking

Generally, the compulsions that you marked on the SOC-OCD are the behaviors and mental activities that you must give up.

Physical and Mental Compulsions

While obsessions are automatic and uncontrolled, compulsions are voluntary actions that are under your control. Just as you can control the movement of your muscles, you can control the performance of physical rituals. The same is true for mental rituals; they are willful words that you say to yourself and images that you purposely produce. The question isn't, "Can I prevent rituals?" but, "Am I willing to prevent them?" If you wish to overcome OCD, the answer must be "yes." The price you'll pay for giving them up—short-term anxiety—is well worth the long-term benefit of freedom from OCD. Clearly the major rituals, washing and cleaning, must be prevented. There are two ways of effectively achieving this.

The first way is to practice reasonable washing and showering (the details are spelled out in chapter 5). This means hand washing only after using the toilet, before preparing meals or eating, or if they are noticeably soiled, and only one ten-minute shower per day. Any washing for the purpose of bringing down distress triggered by contamination fears is not allowed. Doing this only serves to strengthen your OCD by blocking exposure to obsessions, which is the primary requirement for recovery.

The second method is to be used if you're not getting results from reasonable washing, or if you're washing more frequently than allowed. This method requires three days of no washing activities whatsoever, followed by a ten-minute shower on the fourth day. On the non-washing days, no contact with water is permitted, except for drinking and brushing teeth. Shave with an electric shaver. After-shave lotions, body lotions, powders, deodorants, and other toiletries are permitted, provided they are not used for blocking obsessional fears. If you have accidental contact with water, immediately recontaminate yourself and continue the no-washing period until the scheduled shower day. If you must clean something for reasons other than avoiding contamination, use rubber gloves, and when you finish, recontaminate yourself. I realize all of the above seems daunting; however, several of my patients found relief from the prohibition on washing and cleaning, and were even reluctant to resume normal washing, fearing that it could lead to their resumption of compulsive washing—which doesn't happen. Remember the old saying, "It's easier than you think," which has been found true by all the courageous people who have abandoned washing and cleaning rituals and overcome their suffering. You can be one of them. And keep in mind that by shaping your exposures, you can control your anxiety level, which will make it easier to relinquish the rituals.

Distraction

Distraction is probably one of the first false fear-blockers people use to cope with obsessions. By trying to get their minds on something else, they hope to ignore obsessions with their attendant anxiety and distress. Really paying attention to what they're doing, constantly being busy, and keeping on the move are ways those of an energetic bent may use to compete with repetitive, intrusive thoughts and images. Listening to music or chattering incessantly and mindlessly are resorted to by others attempting to dampen the impact of obsessions. Those with the tendency to worry may even concentrate on troublesome problems of everyday life in an effort to push obsessions out of their mind. The most drastic, and decidedly dangerous, distraction is inflicting self-injury, frequently to the head, as if to drive out demons, expiate guilt, or exchange physical pain for emotional anguish. Distractions, like their fear-blocker cousin compulsions, only offer an unpredictable, short-term reduction of the distress inevitably recurring with obsessions. Distractions must be abandoned for the genuine fear eradicator—exposure—to treat OCD effectively.

Avoidance

By now you know how important exposure is for recovery, so you can understand how its opposite—avoidance—prevents recovery. Prior to having this knowledge, however, you did what came naturally and stayed away from triggers that activated irrational thoughts, images, and impulses. Now, you need to take the path to recovery, the one that follows the fear. If you stray from it and wander into the wasteland of avoidance, your journey will be without end. Or as one of my patients said, "I get it, the idea is to be like a heat seeking missile, fix on the fear, follow it, and blow it up."

Avoided situations can be your ally when you recognize that they are actually triggers for your obsessions, and as such, targets for desensitization. When they have been neutralized, and you are able to easily approach them, you will have demonstrated the ultimate proof of a successful treatment outcome.

Reasoning

One of the conditions for being diagnosed with OCD is that the person realizes, most of the time, their fears are unreasonable. However, during severe OCD spikes, this realization is weakened and doubts arise that the dreaded thoughts could be real. For example, could the thoughts really mean that you are:

- Somehow destined to be ill and diseased

- Basically unhygienic

- Responsible for shielding others from contamination

- At risk of losing control of your behavior and emotions

Just as nature abhors a vacuum, humans abhor uncertainty. We deal with it by rationalizing, analyzing, intellectualizing, theorizing, and using all kinds of mental manipulations attempting to achieve certainty.

This happens in OCD when the false fear-blockers of reasoning—"thinking things through"—and challenging irrational thoughts are called into play. As you already know, these efforts at relief are futile. We have little direct control over our emotional reactions because emotions happen to us, they're not things we will to happen. Our rational control of fear is weak, but fear can easily hijack rational control, and does so routinely in OCD. This is because the connections from the brain's emotional systems to the rational systems are stronger than connections from the rational systems to the emotional systems (LeDoux 1996). Philosophers, poets, and other sages have expressed this understanding over the centuries, and joining them today are neuroscientists reporting discoveries from brain imaging studies and innovative experimental techniques about how the brain works. Remember, with fear, what you *think* won't help you, but what you *do* will.

Reassurance Seeking

One of the most powerful and underestimated of these fear-blockers is reassurance. It's a form of compulsion, and I've found it in over 90 percent of the people I've worked with. Because so many compulsively seek reassurance to calm their OCD anxiety, it deserves special attention.

People with OCD worry that their obsessions might come true. To ease this distress they ask other people, usually family members or close friends, over and over again to reassure them that their fears will not materialize. Because obsessions are always unrealistic, the family members or friends (and even therapists) tell them there is no need to worry; nothing bad is going to happen. For instance, it is quite common for people with fears of contamination to seek reassurance that they won't suffer unending anxiety or come down with a fatal disease if they don't wash or clean. Typically they get the reassurance they want and temporary relief, but like other compulsions, reassurance blocks recovery. This is the first paradox of reassurance. Reassurance is not helpful—it's harmful. However, the short-term relief it provides is rewarding enough to keep the person repeatedly seeking more, which is the second paradox. The more reassurance is received, the more reassurance is wanted. Trying to satisfy the demand is like trying to fill a bottomless pit.

In addition to hindering recovery, incessant requests for reassurance can grow to be overbearing demands that lead to interpersonal strife. In one case, after a man's demands became so intense and frequent, that his wife actually moved out and rented an apartment of her own. The two then entered an intensive treatment program where both were helped and the reassurance stopped. This is an example of the third paradox. Once reassurance is eliminated, the reassured finds no further desire for it. This is accompanied by a decrease in their obsessions and other compulsions. How, then, should you handle your urges to ask for reassurance?

First: Simply Stop

Stop asking for reassurance. Identify your most frequent questions and do not ask them. Avoid subtle, indirect ways of getting reassurance. These may be unknown to the reassurers, but knowingly practiced by you. For example, one client I worked with would abruptly stop doing whatever she was doing, sit down, and space out. Her husband learned that these behaviors signaled that she was caught up in obsessions, and unbeknownst to him, they became a nonverbal request for reassurance that he would immediately provide. It was his cue to tell her not to worry, that her fears were irrational, and that it was only her OCD. So, in addition to attending to the obvious requests, subtle, indirect ones also need to be stopped.

Second: Educate Others

Educate your significant others about the harmful effects of reassurance. Have them read this passage. Explain that providing reassurance interferes with recovery.

Third: Create a Gentle Refusal Statement

At first, you will continue to seek reassurance despite your efforts to abstain. Therefore, those people from whom you typically get reassurance need to work with you to create a palatable way to say no. One way of doing this is to say, "I think you're asking for reassurance. Remember, reassurance is not helpful; it's harmful. Therefore I'm not going to respond." However, it's possible that the agreed upon statement itself can become reassuring. Or, it may lead you to believe that nothing bad will happen because the reassurer would warn you if it were. In this case, the best way to end the cycle is for both parties to stop talking about OCD entirely.

Now let's see how Betty did with ritual prevention.

■ Betty's Story: Ritual Prevention

Betty's ritual prevention was to refrain from washing until she felt little or no urge to wash, that is when her SUDS level reached 0 or close to it. She managed to do this despite having urges to rinse her hand "just for a few seconds." When she refrained from washing rituals, she substituted mental ones by going over reasons why her fears were unrealistic. She would remind herself that it was probably OCD and nothing else, and after repeating this like a mantra, the fear would weaken and, unknown to her, so would the benefits of exposure. Her therapist, on learning this, instructed her to refrain from using these false fear-blockers, as they were as detrimental to her recovery. She also revealed that her husband was providing her with regular reassurance by praising her for doing the exercises, which was good, but reminding her that she had nothing to fear, which was an unsolicited fear-blocker. When the deleterious consequences of both these activities—mental compulsions and reassurance—were eliminated, Betty's progress dramatically increased.

AWARENESS

I guess everybody's heard that you must face your fears to overcome them. That's easy to say but hard to do. Our instinctive reaction to threat is fight or flight. This reaction has survival value for dealing with true dangers, but not for the false dangers you fear from OCD. Survival for you is overcoming OCD, which requires experiencing the fear, sticking with it, immersing yourself in it, and subduing it. Reading this may stoke anticipatory fears, but keep in mind that you can use shaping to control your fear levels by approaching the triggers gradually so that you feel only mild to moderate levels of anxiety. On making contact, you might notice that the fear gradually rises but then levels off, and after a while begins to decrease. It is during this last phase that you are getting the benefits of treatment. You are being desensitized.

While facing the fear, your task is to pay attention to your uncomfortable thoughts as well as emotional and physical sensations. Dwell on the scary thoughts and images. Do the opposite of what you've been doing, and accept the fears as being possible. Imagine the dreaded future events happening. Say to yourself, "So be it." Concentrate on the prospect of living in a world of uncertainty, of never knowing if and when something bad is going to happen, of never getting over the anxious condition, and so forth and so on. Keep thinking about thoughts and calling up images to deliberately provoke fear. In this way you are using fear to fight fear. You can't overcome fear by trying to go around it—only by going through it. Really be aware of the emotions you are experiencing.

Also notice your body's physical reactions. Where do you feel the anxiety in your body? If your heart is beating faster and harder, tune in to it. If you have muscle tension, focus on it. If you're breathing faster and harder, notice it. Is your stomach and chest tight? Do you feel hot? Are you sweating? If the answer is yes, it means that you're on the right track because you're feeling the fear and letting it burn itself out. By pursuing the fear, you're destroying it. Exposure is to obsessions and compulsions as sunlight is to vampires. All of these bad feelings are for the good. You'll know this for yourself when, after several exposures, the fear no longer exists. You won't be able to summon it even if you try.

However, you might be concerned that the obsessions will become stronger if you give up your efforts to stop blocking them or if you deliberately bring them on. Or, you might worry that whatever you dread will happen. Paradoxically, neither of these outcomes occurs. Instead, the exact opposite happens; you will recover as a result of retraining your brain's fear system to stop creating false alarms about harmless events. You will be desensitized to the previous fear triggers and see them as they truly are—harmless thoughts and images that are simply part of the normal flow of your stream of consciousness. In other words, OCD is erased when the unwanted thoughts, images, and impulses are faced, and embraced.

You may ask, "If exposure to fear is all that's required to get over OCD, why hasn't this already happened? I've had these obsessions for many years and they just keep coming." The answer is that you have used false fear-blockers to cut off distress from the obsessions so that the exposures to the fear haven't been long enough for it to naturally drop, which it will, simply as a result of your feeling it. You will fully understand the truth of this after you've completed your first exposure exercise.

■ Betty's Story: Awareness

During her first ERPA exercise, Betty had mild to moderate anxiety, increased heart and respiration rates, and sweating. Her SUDS level was about 20, which was a surprise to her, because she anticipated more distress than that. This expectation is quite common and keeps people from testing out situations to see if they are really as bad as they think they are. Nevertheless, it was stressful enough to produce feelings of dread and nervous physical sensations. Betty was able to focus on them, for the most part, and force herself to imagine the worst: that somehow she would contract HIV from the chair. When she caught herself trying to neutralize these fears with reason or distractions, she immediately returned to dwelling on the negative. She also tuned in to her heart rate as it was accelerating and her rapid, shallow breathing which was quite strong. The perspiration on her forehead was quite noticeable at first as was its absence when she became less anxious. The feeling of a coating-like substance on her hand was hard to describe, but it was a good barometer of desensitization because as the sensations faded, so did her fear.

As she continued practicing ERPA, she felt the distressing physical and emotional sensations wither during each practice session, from day to day. This rewarded her, as would the alleviation of any long-standing misery.

Summary

In this chapter, we learned the basics of ERPA and discussed some of its finer points. In the next chapter, we will design your first exposure exercise. It will follow the same steps carried out by Betty:

- Select an obsession-compulsion combination for elimination.

- Practice exposure by bringing on the obsessions in reality and in imagination.

- Practice ritual prevention by refraining from doing compulsions and fear-blocking behaviors.

- Practice awareness by fully experiencing the triggered thoughts, images, impulses, and the feelings they set off.

CHAPTER 5

Exposure Exercises for Fear of Anxiety and Illness

In this chapter, we're going to develop exposure exercises to eliminate washing triggered by fears of dirt, germs, and other hazardous substances. We'll be making use of the techniques covered in chapter 4 by putting them together to make comprehensive, easy-to-use exercises. The next chapter will cover exercises for compulsions triggered by the fear of urine and feces. The one after that will be devoted to the fear of blood. Some readers will have symptoms in just one of these categories, while others will have symptoms in all of them. By performing the exercises you are about to learn on a regular basis, you will be well on your way to recovery. Before getting into the nuts and bolts of the exercises, let's start with a brief discussion about what recovery from OCD means.

RECOVERY

One way to determine if people have recovered from OCD is to evaluate their symptoms after treatment to see if they still meet the requirements for having the disorder. According to the DSM-IV (American Psychiatric Association 1994), a diagnosis of OCD requires that a person's obsessions and compulsions must have one of the following characteristics:

■ They must cause marked distress.

■ They must be time-consuming (that is, they take more than one hour a day).

■ They must significantly interfere with the person's interests and routines, occupational or academic functioning, or usual social activities or relationships.

To be recovered means that a person fits the following criteria:

■ Their obsessions or compulsions, if present, are in the mild or subclinical range of severity.

■ They are able to maintain employment or volunteer activity, or pursue educational or training goals.

■ They are capable of pursuing normal interests and routines.

■ OCD symptoms do not interfere with satisfactory family life, social activities, and relationships.

In other words, the recovered person is able to lead a normal life. The complete elimination of symptoms is the goal for most people. To date, there is no solid information on the percentage of people who become completely symptom free, though based on my clinical experience I'm sure some do. Nevertheless, the disorder is generally regarded as chronic, meaning the symptoms can come and go over time, their return usually being the result of various life stresses. There are, however, studies that show that patients who received behavior therapy continue to improve after their formal treatment has been completed (Bystritsky et al. 1996). This is because they continued to use the techniques they learned in treatment to manage their symptoms. They have truly become their own therapist, and so can you.

EXPOSURE EXERCISES IN REALITY

To become your own therapist, practice the following exercises. You will significantly reduce or eliminate worry and rituals about dirt, germs, and other substances you find to be contaminating.

Try This First: Reasonable Washing

A useful strategy for changing any behavior is to start with a simple, uncomplicated method first. If it doesn't work, then try one of the more complex ones that follow. Reasonable washing means eliminating the excessive and irrational activities that go on during compulsive washing. Most people suds and rinse their hands once—for no more than fifteen seconds—before meals, after using the toilet, and when they are noticeably soiled. They are comfortable taking showers of ten minutes or so, usually once a day. Therefore, your goal is to try to wash and shower like them. The following exercise will show you how to gradually eliminate the excessive activities you're now practicing. This method produces rapid results, but whether you can put up with the initial distress and fight urges to give in to your present excesses is the question. You have a good chance for success if your washing compulsions are in the mild to moderate range of severity. The only way to find out is to try it. I've laid out the steps below.

1. Set aside a day devoted to practicing reasonable washing activities. For hand washing, practice the following:

    - Use only soap and water (no other cleaning or sanitizing agents).

    - Wash only before preparing or eating meals, after using the toilet, or when hands are noticeably soiled.

    - Limit washing time to fifteen seconds or less.

- Suds and rinse only once.

- No washing of lower and upper arms.

- Refrain from all physical or mental rituals.

- Get no help from others.

- Dry your hands on a towel you use for at least five days.

- Avoid activities that wet hands (doing laundry, dishes, shaving, or anything else you might do to sneak a hand washing).

- Avoid all substitutes for washing (like hand wipes, Purell, sanitizing sprays, etc.).

For showering, practice the following:

- Take only one shower per day.

- Limit shower time to ten minutes or less.

- Use soap only (no other cleaning or sanitizing agents).

- Refrain from hand washing during the shower.

- Wash all body parts.

- Use nonabrasive washing materials.

- Avoid all activities that wet your body (swimming, running in the rain or sprinklers, or anything else used to sneak a mini-shower).

- Refrain from all physical or mental rituals.

- Get no help from others.

- Dry with a towel you use for at least the next five days.

2. On this first day of reasonable washing, and all subsequent days, it is crucial that you touch and have contact with the items, situations, and events that

trigger urges to wash or shower. This is the exposure part of the therapy. Avoiding contamination blocks exposure, which blocks recovery just as effectively as your washing and showering rituals have. In other words, you will only be substituting avoidance for washing and showering.

3. At the end of the day, congratulate yourself for any successes and start a list of each washing and showering activity that you performed reasonably. For example, if you limited hand washing to fifteen seconds or less, write it down. However, if you washed more times than allowed, do not list it. Your goal is to continue to add exposure activities to your list each day until you're washing and showering reasonably.

4. On the next day, continue performing the reasonable washing and showering activities that you were success-ful with on the first day. Add one or more new, reason-able washing and showering activities. Praise yourself for successes and add them to the list.

5. On the third day, and each day thereafter, continue practicing the reasonable washing and showering activi-ties previously listed, and add new ones.

6. Continue this procedure until you're washing and showering like everybody else.

For example, let's say you decided to work on eliminating the following:

- Hand washings three to five minutes long

- Hand washing ten times a day

- Sudsing and rinsing three times

- Counting while hand washing

- Showering for thirty minutes

- Hand washing in the shower after washing genitals and buttocks

Let's say at the end of the first day you were able to eliminate counting while hand washing. You would congratulate yourself and start your list of successes by writing this down. On the next day you would continue hand washing without counting, and add one or more new items to tackle from your list, possibly sudsing and rinsing only once. Again, if successful, give yourself credit at the end of the day for your accomplishment, and add this to your list of successes while noticing that the list is beginning to grow. Continue this process and you'll be quite comfortable with reasonable washing, have more time for things you want to do rather than have to do, and feel increased confidence and self-esteem.

If the company of another person makes it easier to resist washing or showering because his or her presence guarantees safety, practice the exercise in his or her company. Ask someone who will appreciate the challenge you are undertaking and is supportive but not bossy. Tell the helper to give you only one or two reminders not to wash, absolutely no physical interference, and no criticism if you do wash. He or she can praise you when you succeed, and, if you fail, remind you that tomorrow is another day. While resisting the urge to wash you may want reassurance that whatever you fear as a consequence of not washing won't happen. Do not give in to requesting reassurance or permitting your helper to volunteer it. This is an exposure exercise, so remember to refrain from using any of the false fear-blockers while you resist washing. Avoid mental rituals, reasoning, and self-reassurance. Instead, practice awareness; pay attention to your physical and emotional sensations, anxious thoughts or images, or both. Stay with them as they gradually decrease and eventually disappear.

When you practice awareness you will also be avoiding the false fear-blockers of mental rituals. Practice the following awareness exercise now when you're not in the grip of an obsession and it will help you to practice awareness when you're doing the exercises.

EXERCISE: PRACTICING AWARENESS

The goal of this exercise is to give you practice in noticing the stuff that makes up your inner world—your thoughts, images, emotions, physical sensations, and anything else that makes you aware of your existence. Get comfortable by reclining, or lying all the way down so that your body is totally supported. Close your eyes to cut down on distraction. Then practice paying attention to your inner state without trying to change anything—just notice what's going on inside yourself for about ten to fifteen minutes. Tune in to the following:

- Physical sensations throughout your body (like your heart rate, breathing, muscle tension, or skin sensations)

- Thoughts, images, memories, fantasies, or worries

- Emotions (such as serenity, happiness, excitement, anticipation, anxiety, dread, sadness, or boredom)

- Sounds

- Scents

After dwelling on your inner state, open your eyes and review the experience to identify any unpleasant thoughts, feelings, images, or sensations that you tried to stop, and the means used to do so. Did something disturbing occur to you? Did you then try to get your mind off of it by distraction, rationalization, or using other fear-blocking techniques? If you did, repeat the exercise and this time let any unpleasant experiences happen. Do not stop them. Practice being aware of them and accepting them. This strengthens your ability to notice and tolerate discomfort, which will significantly reduce or even eliminate it. Also, by practicing when obsession-free, you strengthen your competence for awareness when you're experiencing distress from exposure exercises.

When you first practice awareness as part of an exposure exercise, you'll notice a distressing inner world of physical sensations, emotions, thoughts, and images. But as you continue being aware, you'll notice that your inner world changes and becomes one of calmness, uninhabited by distressing thoughts and images. So when practicing the above reasonable washing exercise, use awareness while resisting impulses to wash. It will remove the distress that drives the washing, and thus the washing itself. If the reasonable washing exercise does not work for you, don't be discouraged. Try the next exercise.

EXPOSURE, RITUAL PREVENTION, AND AWARENESS: IN REALITY

You defeat OCD by defying it, disobeying it, and doing the opposite of what it demands. This section shows you how to do this by practicing exposure, ritual prevention, and awareness (ERPA) exercises for eliminating washing and showering rituals triggered by fear of contamination leading to fears of illness or disease or unending anxiety.

Below is a list of common triggers for the fear of contamination. Check any of the items that trigger your contamination fears if you have contact with them. For any situations not listed, check Other, and make a note of what they are.

Common Triggers for Fear of Contamination

☐   Doorknobs

☐   Handles

☐   Handrails

☐   Elevator buttons

☐   TV remotes

☐   Telephones

☐   Pens or pencils others have used

☐   Books, magazines, or newspapers

☐   Furniture

☐   Tabletops and other surfaces

☐   Sinks

☐   Faucets

☐   Toilet flushers

☐   Toilet seats

☐   Toilet paper

☐   Wash cloths and towels

☐   Dirty clothes

☐   Shoes

☐   Bottom of pant leg

☐   New clothes before washed

☐   Medicine

☐   Certain food or drinks

☐   Animals or insects

☐   Doctors' and dentists' offices, clinics, hospitals, or health-care workers

☐   Certain people

☐   Wastebaskets, trash cans, or garbage cans

☐   Sidewalks, floors, and things that fall on them

☐   Other

_____

_____

EXERCISE: BASIC ERPA

1. Review the triggers for fear of contamination you checked above and choose one of the mild triggers to work on first. For example, let's say it's touching a doorknob that only a few people use.

2. Over the next few days, make note of how many times you avoid it or do washing rituals after contact with it.

3. Choose a day to begin practicing ERPA.

4. On your ERPA day, start the exercise by touching the doorknob fully with the palms and fingers of both hands. This will cause mild to moderate anxiety and

the urge to wash. Instead, stay in contact until you feel some decrease in your distress and then touch many other objects in your surroundings to deliberately "spread" whatever it is that you fear is on your hands.

5. Refrain from any washing or cleaning to get relief from your exposure to contamination. Avoid using any of the mental rituals you checked in chapter 3, such as distraction, reasoning, and reassurance seeking. Your anxiety to wash may increase slightly but will eventually level off and then began to decrease.

6. Practice awareness of distressful physical sensations, thoughts, and images you're experiencing while you refrain from washing. You'll have urges to wash to get relief from the fear that you're going to become ill or contract a fatal disease. Or you could worry that unless you ritualize, your high anxiety will not end and may even drive you crazy. If your heart rate increases and you have tightness in your chest or other muscle groups, pay attention to it. Be aware that these emotional and physical responses are a result of your OCD, and by facing and embracing them you will erase them. As you continue practicing awareness of the distress you'll notice it decreasing on its own, without the need for washing. You are being desensitized.

7. When your SUDS level is 0, or close to it, repeat contact with the item and again practice steps 4, 5, and 6.

8. Practice this exercise as frequently as possible until contact with the item causes no distress.

9. Continue having contact with this item and choose one or more additional low-level items on your list of common triggers for fear of contamination. Do the ERPA exercise to neutralize them. Then practice exposures to the moderate and severe items to eliminate compulsive washing after contact with all of them.

The following are some additional ways you can practice ERPA exercises. Read them over and select those that address your particular washing patterns. You'll get the best results from exercises you practice frequently. It's best to start with the easiest one, and after it no longer poses a problem, try the next easiest one. Continue in this way until you have completed the most difficult exercise, which will then be much easier because your desensitization will be well underway.

EXERCISE: ELIMINATING SEPARATE WASHING ACTIONS ONE AT A TIME

If your washing includes several separate actions, you can eliminate them one by one. For example, when hand washing, Betty would wet her hands, dispense as much liquid soap into her cupped left palm as it would hold, and then clasp her hands and alternately rotate them one over the other up to ten times, always stopping on an even number. Next she washed each finger individually, and then rinsed. She repeated lathering and rinsing two or three times depending how anxious she was to begin with. Each washing episode took up to ten minutes until she felt it was done just right. She gradually eliminated these rituals by stopping one compulsion at a time. First she stopped using excessive soap by pumping the soap dispenser only twice, but she continued the ritualistic hand and finger washing and the repeated lathering and rinsing she had been engaging in. She became accustomed to this change fairly soon, and then gradually reduced rotating her hands, one over the other, to three times (note she stopped on an odd number which flew in the face of OCD that previously demanded she stopped on an even number). Eliminating these rituals caused her fears of contracting AIDS to lessen, and made it easier for her to eventually become comfortable lathering and rinsing only once. Thus she had stopped all three washing actions.

Here are the steps broken down:

1. Choose a washing ritual that involves multiple behaviors.

2. Make a list of the behaviors.

3. Stop doing the easiest behavior first.

4. After you are comfortable with the change, stop doing the next-easiest behavior.

5. Continue the process to eliminate all of the behaviors.

Remember: daily, frequent practice produces the fastest and most satisfying results.

EXERCISE: CHANGING THE ORDER OF WASHING BEHAVIORS

If you wash using a number of actions that must be followed in a certain order, you can disrupt and weaken the ritual by changing the order of the behaviors. For example, when Betty came home from work she always took a shower for at least thirty minutes. During it she washed her body parts always in the same sequence. That is, she would start with her hair and face, followed by her torso, then her legs and feet while avoiding her genital and anal areas. She would then repeat soaping and rinsing all these areas several times, which could take almost a half an hour. Her last behavior was to quickly soap and rinse the avoided body parts and step out of the shower. To get a handle on this considerable problem, Betty started by changing the order of the separate washing actions. This reduced the overall intensity of the urges to ritualize and made it easier for her to steadily eliminate them one by one.

Changing the sequence of washing behaviors may not seem like much of a challenge, but it can have more of an impact than you think. Here are the steps to follow:

1. Choose an activity that involves a particular sequence of washing behaviors.

2. Try a random sequence of washing or reversing the sequence you currently use.

3. If the new routine causes you stress, check your SUDS level and continue the routine until your SUDS level drops.

4. Use some of the above exercises to stop all the ritualis-
    tic washing activities, which will be easier because the
    compulsions will be weakened.

EXERCISE: USING MODELS FOR NORMAL WASHING

Many people who are recovering from compulsive washing are unsure
about how much effort they should devote to washing sufficiently.
They can be aware that they have been excessively concerned about
cleanliness and have spent more time and effort washing than most
people. But they're not sure about how much is enough. If you share
these concerns, seek recommendations from friends or family members whom you regard as practicing good personal hygiene. You can
also use them as models by having them actually demonstrate hand
washing and showering. Observe them as they go through all the
steps involved in a routine washing and daily shower. Then practice
and imitate their behaviors, and they will become your behaviors as
well. Soon you'll feel more natural and free from the false fears of
OCD.

EXPOSURE, RITUAL PREVENTION, AND AWARENESS: IN IMAGINATION

In this chapter so far, I have presented a number of exercises for eliminating washing and showering compulsions. All of these exercises have
involved exposure to the triggers for your rituals that exist in reality. In
the remainder of this chapter I'll present exercises to desensitize you to
triggers that exist only in your mind.

There are two types of exposure activities. One is technically
called *in-vivo exposure* or exposure in reality, because it requires
making contact with real life situations that trigger your contamination fears. The other is called exposure in imagination. It is used for
situations that exist only in the mind about future dreaded consequences that are impossible or highly improbable. Examples are fears
of high, unending anxiety, going crazy, contracting illness or disease,

and even death. Take, for instance, the fear of contracting HIV/AIDS. Practicing exposure in imagination to this fear would mean focusing on thoughts and images of going through the entire process of worrying about having possible symptoms, receiving a diagnosis of HIV/AIDS, undergoing grueling treatments that fail, being hospitalized, and even dying. Include all the particular torments you imagine during such an ordeal.

Another use for exposure in imagination is to make exposure in reality to a particular trigger easier by first practicing exposure to it in imagination. Do these by imagining yourself confronting the contaminated situation while refraining from rituals and practicing awareness. When imagined scenes lose their emotional impact, you can then confront the trigger in reality with less distress.

The technique I'm about to describe may sound really scary and difficult, but it works. To do exposure exercises in imagination, you must complete the following steps:

1. Deliberately trigger obsessions and pay attention to them for extended periods of time.

2. Focus on your emotional and physical reactions and the ensuing thoughts, images, and impulses.

3. Refrain from taking the edge off of the distress by using compulsions or the false fear-blockers of mental rituals, rationalization, counting, or distractions.

4. Notice the decline and eventual absence of distress as you practice the exposure and neutralize fear triggers.

However, you, as most people with OCD, are probably afraid to do this. Imaginal exposure is safe and will help you overcome your fears in the long run. As you begin to face your fear, remember these important points:

1. Deliberately focusing on your obsessions will not make them worse, but instead will weaken them.

2. Consciously thinking about your fears will not make them come true, but instead will make you realize they are ridiculous.

3. The exposure will not cause unending anxiety or insanity, but instead will free you of fear.

4. You will not become so relaxed that you will neglect normal hygienic practices.

Furthermore, imaginal exposure is essential for recovery since there is no effective psychotherapeutic substitute for it. The benefits have been confirmed by several research studies (Foa et al. 1980). Naturally, you might be reluctant to deliberately dwell on the distressful thoughts and images that are at the heart of your disorder. Hundreds of times I have seen anxious apprehension in my patients when I propose the use of this method, which is distressing to witness. However, these initial moments of discomfort pale in comparison to the tremendous relief and emotional highs we both enjoy resulting from their practice of imaginal exposure.

Remember that OCD is a disorder of paradoxes. For instance, obsessions are strengthened when you practice avoidance of their distressful content, and they are only weakened when you consciously entertain their fearful thoughts and images. Keep in mind that the fears are totally unrealistic and hence harmless. But this knowledge alone is powerless, which is another paradox: what you *know* won't help you. Then there's a third paradox. Fear is actually our friend when it warns us of realistic threats to our survival so we can take appropriate actions to steer clear of them. But, paradoxically, when fear is irrational, instead of avoiding it we must face it and embrace it to erase it. By avoiding OCD fears, you ensure they remain a threat. Paradoxically, when you confront these fears, you ensure their demise. Here are some ways to practice imaginal exposure.

Exposure should include the following three parts:

- The content of your obsessions; the thoughts, images, and impulses that drive them

- The dreaded outcome of your obsession, or the perceived consequences

- What your obsessions mean about you as a person

Exposure in imagination, using shaping, can be done with the following tools:

- Written scenarios

- Audiotaped scenarios

- Rereading and rewriting

- Spontaneous obsessions

- Words

- Images

- News reports

- Videotapes and DVDs of movies

ERPA in imagination works the same way as ERPA in reality except the fears you face will be those that take place in your inner world—thoughts and images—instead of events that take place in the physical and social environment. These fears come from worries you have about the problems that coming in contact with contamination or not washing or showering sufficiently could cause. The tools listed above will trigger different levels of distress in different people. Some people are more affected by what they see, whereas others can be more troubled by what they hear. Start with the exercises that are the easiest for you, and gradually take on more difficult ones.

EXERCISE: RECORDING THE FEAR ON PAPER OR TAPE USING SCENARIOS

One of the best ways to do ERPA in imagination is by writing down the content of your obsessions, then recording this scenario on audio-tape and listening to it repeatedly for as long as it takes to feel some relief. You can also practice exposure to the scenario by rewriting and rereading it for extended periods of time, again, until you feel your distress decline. Try both ways, and use the one that works best for you.

Writing the scenario. Think about situations that trigger obsessions or fears of high, unending anxiety or illness and disease. Choose one with a SUDS level in the low to middle range of intensity, and then write about it in the first person, as if it were happening now. Give a detailed and complete description of it including all of these elements:

- The events leading up to the scene

- The setting in which it takes place

- Your activities and physical movements

- Frightening consequences (such as high, unending anxiety; a major mental illness; coming down with the flu or other minor illness; contracting a major illness such as HIV, AIDS, cancer; or contracting other potentially fatal diseases)

- Scary thoughts and images (like confinement in a mental institution, pain and suffering, excruciating treatments, hospitalizations, poor odds for survival, abandonment, or death)

- What you see (for example, the color and movement of things or people's expressions and actions)

- What loved ones, friends, or acquaintances might think and say about you

- What you might feel (like temperature, humidity, pain, being touched)

- What you might smell (such as the odor of mental institutions, hospitals, clinics, or doctors' offices)

- Your emotions (such as fear, apprehension, guilt, sadness, embarrassment, shame, anger, disgust, or despair)

- Feared consequences (like being blamed, criticized, rejected, punished, or pitied by others)

- Your fears of what the obsessions mean about you as a person

- Your bodily responses (like muscle tension, chest and abdominal pain, rapid heartbeat and breathing, sweating, hot and cold flashes, dizziness, or trembling)

Do not include reassuring statements that could serve as false fear-blockers or any other words or phrases that could offer relief. Instead, give the scenario an uncertain or tragic ending.

Once you have completed the scenario, you should repeatedly write and then read it for thirty to ninety minutes, once or twice daily, stopping only after you feel a noticeable decrease in distress.

The following is a scenario written by Betty.

■ Betty's Story: An Imaginal Scenario

I'm driving home, a forty-five-minute trip, and can hardly wait to get to the bathroom. I have been holding my urine all day even though I know it could cause another bladder infection. But I cannot stand the idea of using a public toilet, especially after brushing against that patient in the hospital hallway. Who knows what disease she had. She contaminated my scrubs, and I've had to keep from touching them all day. Sometimes I'd forget about it, and wonder if maybe I did touch them. Did I or didn't I? I just don't know. What if I did? That means I could have touched my face and other parts of myself with contaminated hands. I could be covered with microscopic specks of blood. It doesn't make sense, but I feel like I'm in danger of getting HIV. I've got to get out of these clothes, wash my hands, pee, and shower as soon as I get home. It feels like my bladder is going to burst. I don't think I can hold it much longer. The possibility of HIV is making me feel more and more anxious. Here I go again, my heart is pounding, I'm starting to hyperventilate and sweat, and my muscles are tight. I see myself in the doctor's office; he's telling me that I have HIV. Other thoughts and images are coming in of being treated; the sorrowful look on Juan's face as he tries to be encouraging. I feel guilty, because I might have put him at risk for infection. I'm trying to block the images out, but they keep coming. I know I'm speeding and can't afford any more speeding tickets. So what, I've got to get home. But it's probably too late now. There is probably nothing that can be done. When or will this ever end?

Audiotape exposure. Dictate your written scenario into a tape recorder. The best way is to record it on a three-minute, endless-loop audiotape. A tape of this type automatically repeats the recorded message over and over when you press your recorder's "play" button. By freeing you from the need to rewind and replay your scenario for prolonged exposure to it, you will be able to devote your undivided attention to the exposure activity.

To get the most from your exposure, use these guidelines:

■   Listen to your tape in solitude while reclining comfortably with your eyes closed.

■   Refocus your attention on the tape when you notice that your mind is not on it.

■   Don't engage in any fear-blocking behaviors.

■   Practice awareness of your anxious emotions, bodily sensations, and fearful thoughts and images and the way they gradually fall off as you become desensitized.

■   Continue the exposure exercise until you feel a noticeable drop in your distress.

Stopping while your tension is up can maintain or worsen your fears. Typical exposure periods are thirty to ninety minutes. Do the exposure once or twice daily, including weekends and holidays. As you continue practicing, the trigger weakens and eventually loses its power to provoke stress. This exercise may sound hard, and in the beginning it might be. But as you continue working with it, you will start to enjoy feelings of relief. You will come to know that you are controlling fear that once seemed completely unmanageable. And as your fear decreases, your belief in its reality decreases as well. Keep on keeping on!

EXERCISE: HOLDING ON TO SPONTANEOUS OBSESSIONS

After you've gotten some benefit from the above methods, try doing the exposures by deliberately thinking about and visualizing the content of your obsessions without relying on the written scenarios. Also, when conditions permit and you have a spontaneously occurring obsession, go ahead and dwell on it. Use the same procedure that you do when practicing planned exposures. This is the highest level of exposure and results in the maximum benefits. After you've become desensitized to the first trigger, choose another one to work on using this procedure. Continue zeroing in on them until they're all neutralized.

EXERCISE: FOCUSING ON WORDS

Individual words that are associated with or embodied in your obsessions can also work to promote desensitization. People with washing and cleaning rituals can become sensitized to words that remind them of their fears and are now part of their obsessions. Words that are common triggers include:

- References to bodily substances—blood, saliva, perspiration, feces, urine, semen, or mucus

- References to minor and major illnesses—colds, flu, West Nile Virus, HIV, AIDS, STDs, cancer, mad-cow disease, or other life-threatening illnesses

- References to health-care facilities and health-care professionals

- References to disease-spreading agents

- References to toxic substances and environmental contaminants

- Certain people

- Things people touch

- Household items

This is only a partial list. You can probably come up with additional words that are associated with the disasters that you fear. To do exposure, write words that cause a reaction on slips of paper and post them all around your living quarters, in places where you will frequently see them. An equally effective technique is to repeatedly rewrite and reread lists of trigger words. You can also dictate them on an audiotape and listen to them for prolonged periods of time.

To make this exercise easier, arrange the words in order from low to high distress. Then start your exposures with the easiest word, and once you've been desensitized to it, take on the next word. In this way move through the entire list until you've neutralized the most fearful word. Remember to refrain from rituals, practice awareness, and continue the exposures long enough to feel a noticeable drop in your distress.

EXERCISE: FOCUSING ON IMAGES

Photographs and pictures in magazines, newspapers, and books are a source of fear triggers that can be extinguished by ERPA. Find images related to your fears that you don't like or want to look at because they're related to your fears. Arrange them in order from lowest to highest distress, and, starting with the easiest one, look at them for prolonged periods of time while doing ERPA. Once you have become desensitized to the first one, move to the next, and in this way neutralize all of them. You'll find that this exercise will reduce your distress from spontaneously occurring obsessions and triggers for them.

EXERCISE: USING NEWS REPORTS

Reports of tragedies and disasters in newspapers, magazines, and on television can be a good source for exposure exercises, especially if you have been diligently avoiding them. Actively seek them out and immerse yourself in them. Again, use shaping to start with exposures that are of mild to moderate distress and work your way through more difficult ones. Do this by cutting out and repeatedly reading and examining articles about illnesses and life-threatening diseases, environmental hazards, toxic waste, and so forth. In other words, focus on news reports about problems that relate to your fears of contamination. Do the same with television news reports by habitually watching the evening news and listening to news broadcasting stations on the radio while driving. If you fear being ambushed by unexpected TV or radio news items, stop listening to the radio and start videotaping the news.

This way you can preview various stories and view them according to the level of distress they trigger. After your sensitivity has been decreased sufficiently, practice watching live TV news and listening to the radio news broadcasts.

EXERCISE: WATCHING MOVIES ON VIDEOTAPE AND DVD

A huge number of Hollywood movies contain scenes which will trigger your obsessions. Obtain these films on videotape or DVD and locate the scenes that trigger your fears. Then repeatedly view them in the same way that audiotape exposure is done. That is, rewind and replay a scene until it fails to provoke distress. If there are several scenes in a film, do ERPA with each scene using shaping. No matter how terrifying a scene may be at first, it will become absolutely boring with repeated exposure. Furthermore, you'll notice that the obsessions it triggers are just thoughts and nothing more.

Summary

In this chapter, you have been presented with ERPA exercises to target fear of contamination that triggers compulsive washing. The following chapters will teach you to use some of the same strategies to neutralize other triggers for compulsive washing.

CHAPTER 6

Exposure Exercises for Fear of Urine and Feces

Ironically, three of the most common triggers for compulsive washing are substances from the human body: urine, blood, and feces. These bodily products become regarded as dangerous and are avoided at great cost by many people who compulsively wash. They are feared as sources of imagined microscopic specks of germs and disease that have been spread everywhere, on everything, by those who do not wash after using the toilet or who are suspected of having AIDS. People who see the world in this light diligently avoid contact with common ordinary objects, situations, and people, and ritualize when contact can't be averted. This chapter will teach you how to have direct contact with urine and feces without fear. Think of the benefits you'll enjoy when you're free to touch, feel, handle, and have full body contact with everything you now evade without paying the penalties of fear and ritualizing.

URINE

Most people think of urine as something that's dirty, but really it isn't. It's a waste product secreted by the kidneys that is a yellow to amber-colored, slightly acidic fluid discharged from the body through the urethra. Normal urine is sterile; it contains no bacteria. I was surprised to learn that during combat, medics have used urine to clean their hands when other sanitary means were unavailable. Knowing this won't disabuse you of your fear, which is again evidence that what you *know* won't help you. It's what you do that will—starting with the following exercises.

EXPOSURE EXERCISES IN REALITY

To become your own therapist, practice the following series of exercises which will give you step-by-step directions for slowly, but surely, having direct contact with urine. By doing so, you'll significantly reduce or eliminate worries and rituals that are produced by this truly harmless liquid.

EXERCISE: WRITING, READING, AND HEARING THE "U" WORD

People who are sensitized to urine fears can find it difficult to see, say, or hear the word "urine" and words associated with it. If you're one of them, you're probably already anxious from having just read so much about it. If so, reduce your sensitivity by following these steps:

1. Schedule at least thirty minutes to practice this exercise one or more times each day.
    Betty scheduled 30 minutes each morning before work to work on her urine fears.

2. Practice exposure by repeatedly writing long lists of the word "urine" and any other words associated with it that trigger urges to wash. When your list has filled the sheet, read it aloud into a tape recorder and listen to it.

In this way, continue writing, reading, recording, and listening to the words.

Betty wrote the following list: urine, urinate, urinating, urinated, urinal, take a leak, pee, peeing, peed, piss, pissed off, toilet seat, toilet paper, bladder infection, urologist.

3. Practice ritual prevention by not washing, cleaning, or using any false fear-blockers. Washing is allowed only when it is not used as a ritual.

    At first Betty had mild to moderate urges to stop the exercise and wash. She also had fleeting thoughts and images associated with HIV infection. But as she continued writing, reading, and listening to the words, the exercise became easier.

4. Practice awareness by paying attention to your feelings, distressing thoughts, images, or urges. Stay with it until you realize that your stress and urges to wash have appreciably decreased. This means you're being desensitized.

    Betty continued working with the words, and when the obsessive thoughts of HIV entered her awareness, she focused on them, noticing her fear and its expression in her bodily sensations.

5. Continue practicing steps 2, 3, and 4 daily until the words provoke no further distress.

    Betty practiced the exercises for three days in a row, and on the fourth day the words didn't bother her at all.

EXERCISE: MAKE SIGNS AND CARRY URINE CARDS

Another way to desensitize yourself to the word, and the fluid itself, is to make small signs by writing the word on pieces of paper and posting these signs around your living quarters where you will frequently see them. You can continue this type of exposure by writing the word on five-by-seven-inch cards, carrying them with you wherever you go, and reading them frequently.

You are now prepared for the next set of exercises that will gradually bring you into direct contact with urine. Don't panic! Remember the fable in chapter 4, "The Lady Who Learned to Love Rats." She was successful because she used small steps to achieve her goal, while avoiding undue distress.

EXERCISE: FAKING IT WITH FOOD COLORING

Even though you know that the triggers for your fear are not truly dangerous, they nevertheless continue to provoke anxiety. This means that even what you know to be irrational does not prevent fear when you are face-to-face with an OCD trigger. This is true for fake triggers as well. As mentioned earlier in the book, when people with OCD are told they are going to be presented with fake blood, they snicker at the idea that it will provoke fear. But they find out that it does provoke fear, though at a lower level than real blood. This means we can use simulated triggers for exposure exercises as a fairly easy starting point for ongoing exposure to the real triggers. To see if this works for you, do the following:

1.   Prepare fake urine by filling a small container about half full with water and dropping two or three drops of yellow food coloring into it (or an amount that will make it closely resemble the color of urine). For a touch of realism you might heat it to body temperature in the microwave.

     Betty filled a measuring cup half full of water and put two drops of yellow food coloring in it. When she swirled it around, she was struck by how much it resembled the real thing. Warming it to body temperature really made it real!

2.   Practice exposure by "contaminating" your fingers and hands with some of the fake urine. Rub it in real good. While your hands are still slightly moist, rub them on your face, clothes—all over. Then spread the contamination by touching everything in your home you've been avoiding or trying not to contaminate. For example, all of your clothes (including the ones you aren't

wearing), dishes and eating utensils, bedding, and door-knobs. In other words, rub it on everything that will cause you distress from contamination. Don't worry about the food coloring staining. It's washable. For prolonged exposure, moisten a wad of tissues with the fake urine, carry it on your person, and handle it until it no longer bothers you.

Betty dipped her index finger into the fake pee and gingerly rubbed it on her left palm. She was surprised at the strength of her reaction to it. She knew it was food coloring and water but it felt like it was real. She wanted to get it off her hands. After a few seconds she pressed her hands together and touched her face with both hands. Then she touched her clothes. She was reluctant to touch things in the kitchen, but she managed to pat the kitchen counter, refrigerator, and table with both hands. She put the urine-stained tissue in her pocket and kept it there all day. It bothered her at first, but as time passed, she felt only occasional small surges of anxiety when she touched it.

3. Practice response prevention by refraining from any washing or cleaning activities or use of false fear-blockers. After your SUDS level has returned to zero or close to it, only then is washing permissible. This may take all day, so start the exercise early on a day when you will not be stressed by other responsibilities. If you do wash, which should be only if your hands are noticeably soiled, immediately recontaminate yourself with the fake urine.

    Betty felt mild to moderate urges to wash, and had occasional thoughts that the liquid was really urine. She even began to mentally review making the fake pee. When she caught herself doing this to get reassurance, she stopped it. She let the doubts come as they may. She was able to refrain from washing until several hours later. When she did, it was to prepare dinner, not to relieve anxiety.

4. Practice awareness by noticing feelings of apprehension and anxiety. Also notice any thoughts and fears of

never-ending distress, having a nervous breakdown, or contracting illnesses or life-threatening diseases. Pay particular attention to urges to wash, and really notice the distress caused by not doing it. This is defying OCD and thereby defeating it. As time passes, you'll notice that your overall distress gradually evaporates.

As the day went on, Betty noticed less distress and fewer thoughts about being contaminated. Her initial SUDS level was about 25, and ten minutes later, it peaked at 35. From then on, there was a downward trend, which reached a low of about 10.

5. Practice steps 2, 3, and 4 one or more times daily until this exercise loses its power to provoke any distress, and has "magically" turned the "urine" into plain old colored water.

In many instances, people with urine fears worry that they have accidentally wet their underwear when they haven't. This triggers compulsions of checking their underwear repeatedly despite never finding evidence of any soiling. If this is the case for you, an additional exercise is to spot your underwear with the fake urine, wear them, and periodically check them. The sight of the stains can trigger obsessional fears and the urge to change underwear and/or wash. Do neither. Instead, just notice the content of your obsessions, the urges to wash or change, and the physical and emotional sensations you experience.

If this exercise caused you no alarm, it means that your fear response to urine is fairly weak. If it caused initial apprehension that dissipated as a result of practice, it means that your desensitization is underway. In either case, do the next exercise.

EXERCISE: THE REAL THING

Now you're ready for contact with actual urine. There are two ways you can do this. The first one gives faster results, but might be harder to do. The second way, using shaping, is easier but will take longer to get results.

The Fast Way

It's natural to have some anxiety about doing this exercise. But don't let it stop you from doing it. Recall the many times you've experienced less anxiety from the actual situation than you experienced anticipating it.

1. Practice exposure by moistening a cloth or wad of tissue with urine and apply it to your hands. Rub them together and then rub your hands on your face and all over your clothes. Follow this by touching many objects in your home. Then spread the contamination by touching everything in your home you've been avoiding or trying not to contaminate. For prolonged exposure, moisten a wad of tissue, carry it on your person at all times, and frequently handle it.

     Betty was somewhat reluctant to start this exercise, but felt good about the ones she had just completed. So she picked a day when she wouldn't be bothered by other things and wet a cloth with a few drops of her urine, then wiped her hands with it. Then she touched her face with her fingers, gently with both hands. She followed this by wiping her hands on all of her clothes. She felt excited because she had done it, and anxious—though not as much she had anticipated— because she wasn't sure what was going to happen.

2. Practice response prevention by refraining from any washing or cleaning activities or use of false fear-blockers. Do no washing or cleaning until you're free from the urge to do them to relieve distress.

     Betty had mild thoughts about possible harmful effects from the urine that caused urges to change clothes and wash. She resisted them with less effort than she had fighting off washing urges following exposure to the fake urine.

3. Instead of washing, practice awareness by focusing on any unpleasant sensations, emotions, or urges to wash or clean. Notice how the distress goes down by itself without the need to do rituals. When this happens, OCD is losing its capacity to control you.

By now Betty was getting good at tuning in to her feelings, bodily sensations, and thoughts which she noticed were in the mild range. Her highest SUDS level was about 25 and she sensed that it would drop fairly quickly if she remained open to the awareness that she was covered with pee.

4.   Practice steps 1, 2, and 3 one or more times daily until the urine causes no more reaction than water does.

Betty practiced this exercise daily, sometimes twice, and in less than a week her SUDS level was at 0 or close to it.

The Slow Way

This exercise allows you to practice gradual exposure by starting with highly watered-down urine and finishing with full-strength urine. That is, the first exposure will be to a very small amount of urine in a lot of water, and you will quickly get used to it. The next solution will be only slightly stronger than the first, and again you will adjust to it. In this way, you will have contact with stronger and stronger solutions of urine and water, pausing at each step and moving on to the next one when you're ready for it. Your final step will be to have contact with pure urine, and it will cause you no more distress than you had at the first step. Note: if your fears are only of other people's urine, this exercise can still help you. So try it before immediately dismissing it. Practice the following exercise one or more times per day:

1.   Urinate in the toilet, don't flush it, and instead use an eyedropper to extract some of the urine that has been diluted by the water in the toilet bowl. Dilute it further by squeezing one drop of it into a pint of water and stir well.

2.   Practice exposure by putting a drop of this very weak pee solution in the palm of your hand. Rub your hands together and spread the contamination on your face and clothes. Then spread the contamination around by touching everything in your home you've been avoiding

or trying not to contaminate, just as you did in the previous exercises.

3. Practice ritual prevention by not washing or using any of the false fear-blockers. When your anxiety level has dropped to where it was at the start of the exercise, it's okay to wash, just as long as it is not a compulsion to reduce anxiety or prevent something bad from happening.

4. Practice awareness by fully paying attention to feelings of distress, uncomfortable bodily sensations, scary thoughts and images, and urges to wash. Stay with it until you notice a considerable decline in these feelings and thoughts. This means that you're being desensitized.

5. Practice steps 1–4 daily until this exercise causes little or no distress.

6. Repeat step 1 but dilute the urine and toilet water solution by putting a drop of it in a half pint of water and stirring it up. Repeat steps 2–4.

7. Continue preparing progressively stronger urine solutions and doing ERPA. When you come to the moment of truth—exposure to full-strength pee—it will be no more difficult than your exposures to diluted urine. There are many ways you can do this. One way is to moisten toilet paper with a few drops of urine and then do ERPA as outlined above. Another way is to collect some urine in a small container and dip your fingers in it or even splash it on your hands and then do ERPA.

8. Prolonged exposure gives the best results from ERPA. Try carrying a tissue moistened with a few drops of urine in your pocket or handbag as you go about your day's activities and frequently handle it.

Completion of this exercise will give you a feeling of relief, because you will have less fear of urine and consequently less concern about it. Also, you'll feel more confident that you can whip this devil, which will make it easier for you to have contact with things you've been avoiding and resist urges to wash. To consolidate your gains, I recommend the following exposure exercises.

EXERCISE: INCREASING FLUID INTAKE AND URINATION FREQUENCY

If you have been avoiding drinking water or other liquids, even when you're very thirsty, so that you don't urinate as much, you're practicing a false fear-blocking. Don't do it: drink at least eight glasses of water per day. In addition to promoting recovery from OCD, you'll be preventing serious physical health problems from the effects of dehydration. When severe, it causes light-headedness, sensations of passing out, and mental confusion. If the dehydration worsens, blood pressure can fall, causing shock and serious damage to internal organs such as the liver, kidney, and brain.

If you're trying to avoid urine by not peeing, you're also practicing false fear-blocking. Give this practice up and urinate from four to six times per day as most people do. Not only will this promote exposure and therefore desensitization to urine, it will also prevent urinary tract infections and serious kidney problems due to the failure of proper bladder emptying (*Merck Manual of Medical Information* 1997).

To change your pattern of insufficient drinking and limited urination, start drinking eight glasses of water per day and urinating at least four to six times during your waking hours as suggested above. If this is more than you can achieve right off the bat, use shaping. Each day gradually increase the amount of water you drink and the number of times you pee. It's been found that keeping a record of the number of times you engage in a behavior you want to do more causes the behavior to increase. So, keep a record of the number of times you drink or pee each day, and take delight in seeing the numbers increase over time.

EXPOSURE EXERCISES IN IMAGINATION

Contact with urine usually triggers fears of something bad happening in the future, such as having unending anxiety that may even build to panic, contracting a serious or fatal disease, or both. Of course, there can be other dreaded consequences that might be unique to the individual. In any case, writing a scenario about the dreaded event and practicing exposure to it by rewriting it or recording it on audiotape will free you from these irrational and fearful obsessions (see chapter 5 for details on doing this). Here is an example of a scenario Betty wrote:

> *I practiced putting urine on my hands and spreading it because I can't continue to have these bladder infections from not using public bathrooms. But now that I've done it, I'm not sure I did the right thing. What if my urine was somehow infected with something I don't know about? I know it's silly, but it feels like it's true. Otherwise why would I be having these thoughts? My heart is starting to beat faster and I'm feeling warm. Worrying about this is making me nervous. Why would this be happening if there was not really something to be afraid of? I probably took a chance that I shouldn't have. Now I'm going to be anxious and worrying for who knows how long. I probably shouldn't have put that pee on myself and everything else. I can't take it back now. I can't undo it. This anxiety is probably just the first of a lot I'm going to have. Why did I do it? What's going to happen? Will I be able to stand it?*

Betty recorded this on audiotape and replayed it repeatedly each day for periods of forty-five to sixty minutes at a time. The first time she listened to it, she had a SUDS level of 40. But with each successive practice session, her anxiety fell, and after five days, the recording caused practically no distress. With this decrease in fear, there was an increase in her conviction that her fears were foolish, and listening to the tape became boring. This exercise stripped the thoughts of their power to dominate Betty's attention, and they became just meaningless flotsam in her stream of consciousness.

FECES

Feces are bodily waste products that are about 75 percent water, the remainder consisting of bacteria, protein, undigested food, fiber, waste material from food, fats, salts, and substances released from the intestines and the liver. Perhaps its repugnant stench is nature's way of keeping us away from it and protecting us from its many parasites, bacteria, and other harmful substances, because failure to heed its odiferous warning can cause real harm. However, OCD exaggerates this threat, turning it into an obsession that triggers avoidance and ritualizing which can take over the lives of those it masters. You can free yourself by doing exercises similar to those that work for fear of urine.

EXPOSURE EXERCISES IN REALITY

The first two exercises below will probably cause only mild to moderate distress that you can eliminate fairly quickly by practicing them on a daily basis. Successfully completing them will also make the rest of the exercises in this chapter easier.

EXERCISE: WRITING, READING, AND HEARING THE "F" WORD

This exercise will desensitize you to seeing, reading, and hearing the word "feces" and its many synonyms, most of which are slang, and other words that you associate with it. Poop, doo-doo, crap, shit, stool, excrement, anus, toilet, and toilet paper are a few examples. If you're not bothered by these words, skip this exercise and consider the one that follows. But if you cringe or even wash when you have thoughts about, hear, or see the poop words, practice the steps in the first exercise in this chapter, "Writing, Reading, and Listening to the 'U' Word," but substitute feces words that bother you for the urine words.

EXERCISE: MAKE SIGNS AND CARRY FECES CARDS

Neutralize the words, and the substance itself, by making small signs with the poop words on them and post them around your living quarters so you'll see them frequently. Extend this exposure outside the home by writing the words on five-by-seven-inch cards, carrying them with you at all times, and reading them frequently.

EXERCISE: VIEWING IMAGES OF FECES

By simply looking at pictures of feces, you will become less sensitive to it. Do this by looking at photographs of feces (take pictures of your pet's or another dog's poop) or scenes in movies on DVDs and videocassettes that depict bathroom activities, for example *Envy* and *Along Came Polly*. You'll also be surprised by what you can find on the Internet. Select pictures that raise your SUDS level to the mild or moderate range, then practice ERPA by setting aside exposure sessions to look at them long enough to cause your initial distress to decrease noticeably. For scenes from movies on DVDs or videocassettes, repeatedly rewind and replay the scene for prolonged viewing. While doing exposures, practice ritual prevention by banishing false fear-blockers from your mind and by refraining from any washing until it's only for the purpose of cleaning and not for anxiety relief. Instead, practice awareness by paying full attention to any distressing thoughts, images, or urges to wash. This exercise will help reduce the difficulty you'll have doing the following exposure activities.

EXERCISE: FAKING IT WITH SIMULATED POOP

This exercise involves exposure to fake feces and will make it easier for you to take on the real thing later. Even though you know the materials you'll be working with are not actual feces, your OCD will react to them as if they were real. Perhaps not as strongly, but enough to desensitize you to them and to actual poop.

Try the following:

1. Go to a novelty store and purchase artificial poop. It comes in a variety of sizes, colors, and shapes. Buy the scariest piece and take it home. Practice ERPA, using the artificial doo-doo instead of the fake urine, by carrying out steps 2, 3, and 4 from the "Faking It with Food Color" exercise earlier in this chapter.

2. An additional way to simulate feces is to repeat the exercise above, but substitute a wad of toilet tissue streaked with brown shoe polish for the artificial poop.

EXERCISE: THE REAL THING

The next step is to address avoidance and rituals associated with bowel movements and then feces itself.

Normal Toilet Hygiene

First we'll start with bowel movements. Do the following:

- If you cover the toilet seat to avoid direct contact with it, practice sitting on it with your bare behind (except when using public toilets).

- If you use gloves or tissues to flush the toilet, practice touching the flusher with your bare hand.

- If you sit on the toilet in the nude so your clothes won't be contaminated, practice using it with your clothes on.

- If you engage in bathroom cleaning rituals before or after bowel movements, give them up.

- If you use laxatives or suppositories to completely empty your bowels because you fear leaking stool, discontinue them.

- If you wipe with voluminous amounts of toilet tissue that causes bleeding or stops up the toilet, or if you take long showers after bowel movements, refrain from these rituals.

- If you try to avoid having bowel movements by restricting your food intake, eating special diets, or retaining your stool, relinquish these practices.

The Final Step

By now you should be ready for the final exposure, contact with feces itself. This can be done safely by following the steps outlined. They will gradually expose you, at your own pace, to direct contact with a very small amount your own feces. If you think about it, we're all exposed to traces of feces every time we have a bowel movement. Theoretically, it's almost impossible to entirely cleanse oneself of microscopic traces of feces. If you, like many of the people I propose this exercise to, object to doing it because it's not normal to practice deliberately touching your own stool, I offer you this: I agree it's not normal, but neither is washing and cleaning compulsively to forestall unrealistic fears of anxiety or catastrophic physical illness from contact with a bodily substance you created. This exercise will free you from *that* abnormal behavior. You can do it gradually, in two stages, or skip the first stage and go directly to the second one. Here's the first stage:

1. Practice exposure by cleaning your anal area in the shower or bath, and after drying, touch a wad of toilet paper to it. Then, as you have done in previous exercises, rub it all over yourself, contaminate your home, and all surfaces and objects you have avoided contaminating.

2. Practice ritual prevention by not engaging in any washing activities or false fear-blockers until you feel no compulsions to do them.

3. Practice awareness by paying attention to the thoughts, feelings, and impulses triggered by the exposure. Stay

with them as best you can and notice their gradual decline as time passes.

4. Repeat this exercise as frequently as possible until it causes no distress.

Here's the second stage:

1. Following a bowel movement, wipe until only a hint of feces is seen on the toilet paper. To make it germ free, spray it with Clorox. When it's dry, practice exposure as described in step 1 in the exercise above.

2. Practice response prevention as described in step 2 in the exercise above.

3. Practice awareness as described in step 3 in the exercise above.

4. Continue practicing the exercise until it causes no distress.

EXPOSURE EXERCISES IN IMAGINATION

Follow the guidelines outlined in chapter 5 for writing a scenario about the content of your obsessions or dreaded outcomes from feces contamination. Rewrite and reread it repeatedly for prolonged periods, or dictate it on an audiotape for extended exposures.

Summary

This chapter presented exercises with an emphasis on direct contact with urine and feces. With sufficient practice, you'll eliminate the basic fear of these substances, objects, and the circumstances associated with them. The net result will be no more avoidance or ritualized washing after contact with the many things that previously triggered fear and subsequent unwanted behaviors. You will have rid yourself of previously feared bodily wastes and your irrational fear will be excreted as well.

CHAPTER 7

Exposure Exercises for Fear of Blood

Fear of blood is one of the most common triggers for washing compulsions even though blood itself is rarely seen by those who fear it. Their apprehension is easily triggered by the mere suggestion of its presence. This is evidenced by their reactions to many things that resemble the real thing, such as red spots on the pavement, stains on napkins and other materials, blemishes, scrapes, scabs, scars, bandages, and any number of things that are misperceived as blood. Like its cousins, urine and feces, microscopic specks of blood, carrying HIV and AIDS and other fatal diseases, are feared to be on almost everything and everywhere, causing sufferers to be hypervigilant in order to avoid them and consequently doomed to anxiety and ritualizing when they can't. You can learn to banish these damnable red flecks from your consciousness and end compulsive washing by practicing the following exercises.

EXPOSURE EXERCISES IN REALITY

You can learn to lose your fear of blood by practicing the following three exercises that will gradually expose you to it.

EXERCISE: READING, WRITING, AND HEARING THE "B" WORD

If you're sensitive to hearing, seeing, or writing the word "blood" or other words that you associate with it (for example, cut, scab, stab, knife, wound, artery, vein, hypodermic needle, scalpel, and so forth), follow the instructions in chapter 6 for the exercise "Writing, Reading, and Hearing the 'U' Word" and substitute the blood words for the urine words. Also practice the "Make Signs and Carry Urine Cards" exercise. Again, substitute the blood words for the urine words. Once you're feeling fairly comfortable seeing, hearing, and saying the blood words, it means you're ready for the next exercise.

EXERCISE: VIEWING IMAGES OF BLOOD AND DISEASE

You can use images of blood and disease to reduce your sensitivity to the bodily fluid and the dreaded consequences of contamination. Good sources are books on anatomy and biology and other medical texts with photographs and drawings of internal organs and other body parts that are both healthy and in various states of morbidity. There are a multitude of films available on videotape and DVD that have one scene after another of blood and gore, as well as plots revolving around AIDS and other terminal illnesses. To desensitize yourself to scenes in the films that are triggers, repeatedly view them and you'll eventually be bored, a state that is incompatible with anxiety. The Internet is also a rich source of illustrations of blood and the consequences of blood-transmitted diseases. These kinds of exposures will reduce your sensitivity to blood as well.

EXERCISE: FAKING IT

Phony triggers easily fake the brain out. It has a hard time telling a real danger from a false one. We can use this information to train the brain to stop setting off false alarms to fake blood, which will in turn help stop the false alarms to real blood. This exercise shows you how to do it.

1. Put a few drops of red ink or food coloring on several sheets of folded tissue. When it's dry, practice exposure by thoroughly rubbing it on your hands, face, and clothes. Then touch the tissue to other things in your household.

   Betty dropped red food coloring on a paper towel and was surprised at the tension she had watching its redness spread. She became even more anxious when she wiped it all over herself. It triggered thoughts of HIV.

2. Practice response prevention by refraining from washing, cleaning, or using false fear-blockers until you're free from any of the urges brought on by this exercise.

   Betty had mild urges to wash, which were easy to resist. She did find herself trying to block out the HIV thoughts, which she stopped doing when she was aware that she was using false fear-blocking.

3. Practice awareness by noticing feelings of fear and worry about disease and illness. Focus on physical sensations that go with your anxiety, such as increases in heart and breathing rates, sweating, and muscle tension. Stay with it as long as it takes to feel a noticeable reduction in your distress level. Desensitization is well underway.

   Betty paid attention to her feelings, thoughts, and bodily sensations while keeping in mind how she smeared herself with "blood." As she did this, relief from anxiety was occurring which felt good.

4. Practice steps 1, 2, and 3 one or more times daily until the exercise provokes no distress and the fake blood becomes just spots of color on tissue.

When you have successfully completed this exercise, you're ready to take on the next one. It involves the use of theatrical blood which actors use for plays and movies, and Halloween revelers use for all kinds of gory, macabre monsters and ghouls. The resemblance between fake blood and real blood is remarkable, which makes it ideal for our purposes. It's available in most novelty shops. Here's how to use it:

1. Place a drop of the fake blood on several sheets of folded tissue.

2. Practice exposure by simply looking at the blood-stained tissue.

3. Practice response prevention by avoiding the use of the false fear-blockers, any washing or cleaning activities, or substitutes for them such as rubbing your hands together.

4. Practice awareness by focusing on emotional and physical distress and urges to wash or look away from the tissue. As time passes, you will notice that your distress is decreasing. Continue this until your SUDS level has noticeably declined.

5. Repeat steps 1–4 until this exercise provokes little or no distress or urges to wash.

EXERCISE: FEAR OF CONTAMINATING OTHERS

If you have fears of contaminating other people, do exposure by touching them while your hands are contaminated with the theatrical blood. Then practice response prevention and awareness as indicated in the above exercises.

EXERCISE: FEAR OF OTHER PEOPLE'S BLOOD

If you're afraid of contact with blood from other people, get the assistance of a helper that knows of your problem and is supportive. Then do the following:

1. Explain the reasoning behind the exercise, and, if necessary, show your helper passages from this book to help them understand what this is all about.

2. Practice exposure by having the person dab some artificial blood on their hands and then shake your hand, touch your face and clothes, and spread contamination throughout your household.

3. Practice response prevention by not washing, cleaning, or using false fear-blockers. Do no washing or cleaning until your SUDS level is at 0 or close to it.

4. Practice awareness by noticing urges to wash and thoughts and images of the impending disease. Notice how your distress goes down on its own, as time passes, without any ritualizing.

5. Repeat steps 2, 3, and 4 until this exercise causes you little or no distress.

EXERCISES FOR FEAR OF BLOOD-TRANSMITTED DISEASES

Complete desensitization requires safe exposure to the top levels of your fear hierarchy. Making direct contact with real blood is not possible because there is no way of determining with certainty that it would be free of disease-causing agents. Besides, it's not blood that's the primary fear. The ultimate fear is of diseases that are transmitted by blood, such as HIV and AIDS. Even other illnesses for which blood is not a vehicle are sometimes feared. Therefore, the following exercises eliminate washing triggers associated with real and imagined diseases from blood contact.

EXERCISE: VISITING HOSPITALS AND AIDS CLINICS

If just the thought of being in a hospital or AIDS clinic makes you nervous, it's a good sign because it means this exercise will work for you. Remember, the anticipatory fear you may be feeling now can be worse than the distress you will actually experience from the exercise. When you finish this activity, you will have scaled a mountain of fear and will be standing on its peak enjoying the view. The next leg of your climb involves using the following handholds and footholds:

1. Pick the easier of the two places to start with, either a hospital or an AIDS clinic, and schedule a day to visit it.

   Betty decided to start with a hospital and scheduled a day to visit it.

2. Practice exposure by visiting the location and walking through hallways, sitting in waiting rooms, handling magazines and handouts (take one home), drinking from water fountains, eating in the cafeteria or snack shop, and using the restrooms. Be sure to touch doorknobs, elevator buttons, and handrails. In other words, contaminate yourself as much as possible. For prolonged exposure, discreetly wipe a tissue on a contaminated item or surface and keep it with you until it stops bothering you. Remain in the location until your SUDS level decreases significantly from the time you entered the location.

   Betty chose to visit a medium-sized hospital. She started her exercise by walking through the hallways and pressing elevator buttons for different floors. These activities caused moderate distress, and after about twenty minutes of doing this her distress dropped to a level where she felt she could sit in a waiting room. When she did, her anxiety increased. So she stayed there for about an hour until it decreased. During this time she looked at magazines and informational materials, one of which she took home. When her anxiety went down to a SUDS level of about 20, she thought about drinking from a water fountain, but couldn't bring herself to do it. Just the idea of it raised her SUDS level, so she returned to the waiting room and stayed there until her SUDS again decreased to about 15. Then she went home. She felt that she had done a pretty good job even though she hadn't eaten in the cafeteria, drunk from the water fountains, or used the restrooms. She decided to try these activities during her next visit.

3. Practice response prevention by refraining from washing or using false fear-blockers.

    Being in the hospital triggered Betty's thoughts of contracting HIV and AIDS. So she tried to ward them off by reading a magazine article. When she realized she was using distraction, she stopped reading and started noticing her surroundings and looking at the people coming and going. She wanted to go home and immediately wash, but she stuck it out.

4. Practice awareness by noticing thoughts, feelings, images, and urges stirred up by being in the situation.

    When Betty stopped using distraction, she started attending to the intrusive images associated with her fear of contracting HIV. She also made herself consciously aware of being in a hospital by noticing the smells, the feel of her chair, the sight of people hurrying about in white coats and green scrubs, and faces reflecting despair, distress, and boredom. As time passed, so did her high level of distress. As it lessened, she felt budding feelings of confidence in her ability to recover.

5. Repeat steps 2, 3, and 4 until you are able to touch everything everybody else does without having obsessions and compulsions.

    Betty repeated her hospital exposure exercises until she had overcome her fears of using the restrooms, drinking from water fountains, and eating in the cafeteria. By then her OCD symptoms were mild and steadily fading. Her next step was to visit an AIDS clinic.

AIDS clinics, being considerably smaller than hospitals, do not afford visitors the anonymity found in large medical centers. But you can still visit one and maintain your privacy. The duration of your visit will be briefer than a hospital visit, but can be just as beneficial. Here's how to do it:

1.   Locate a clinic, and decide on a day to visit it.

     Betty found an AIDS clinic close to her home and decided to go there the next day.

2.   Practice exposure by visiting the clinic. Once you are there, inform the receptionist that you're not seeking an AIDS test but would like to pick up any literature they have on AIDS, its treatment, current research, and so forth. If you have to wait to speak to someone, take this as an opportunity for exposure by sitting in the reception area. Also make discreet contact with as many surfaces, objects, and items as possible. Pick up handouts and browse through them. Take some of them home, and contaminate yourself by rubbing them all over your body and clothing. Then contaminate your living environment by touching the material to everything that you come into contact with on a daily basis.

     On walking up to the entrance, Betty felt her tension rising, and she had second thoughts about touching the door to enter the building. Nevertheless, she did it. She had to wait to speak to a staff person so, after some hesitation, she tentatively sat on the edge of a chair and looked through some handouts. When her turn came, she explained to the receptionist that she was not there for AIDS testing but to get information on AIDS and the clinic's services. A conversation ensued during which Betty managed to place her hands on the counter. She was given more handouts that she put in her bag. She then expressed her thanks and departed. On arriving home, Betty followed through on the rest on the exposure by wiping the AIDS papers on most of the things she touched over a twenty-four-hour period at home.

3.   Practice ritual prevention by not washing as long as you're having thoughts, images, or urges to wash. Do

not use other kinds of behavioral rituals or false fear-blockers to minimize your distress. You may engage in normal washing once you are free of all compulsions dictated by OCD.

After visiting the clinic, Betty didn't wash for the remainder of the day. At first she had sporadic spikes of fear about being exposed to infection. She reacted with mental compulsions, going over reasons it was impossible to contract AIDS by simply being in an AIDS clinic. She recognized this thinking as a futile attempt to block fear and instead just noticed the fearful thoughts. She had periodic urges to wash but successfully resisted them. As the day went on and the fear weakened, her thoughts were less about the clinic and AIDS and more amount everyday life events.

4. Practice awareness by focusing on any distressing feelings, thoughts, images, and urges to wash triggered by the clinic visit. As you continue noticing them, you'll also notice them gradually dwindling.

    Betty practiced awareness by considering the risks she took by being in a place inhabited by AIDS patients who had probably contaminated everything in clinic. She noticed the fright triggered by these considerations and didn't try to block it with self-reassuring statements. Neither did she give in to urges to wash. By the end of the day her distress was almost nil and she was able to sleep well that night.

5. Repeated visits to the same AIDS clinic may be impractical because sooner or later the staff are going to question your reasons for being there since you are not receiving services. Of course, if other AIDS clinics are available, you can visit them and repeat steps 2, 3, and 4. If not, practice step 2 by continuing, on a daily basis, to contaminate yourself and your home environment with the handouts. Then follow steps 3 and 4. Continue these activities until they become boring. By that time you will be completely nonresponsive to what were once potent triggers for compulsive washing.

EXERCISE: DONATING BLOOD

By doing the following exercise, you're helping to save yourself from a life restricted by OCD, and also helping to save the life of someone who needs blood. Donating blood will present an opportunity for you to de-fang the blood devil that's been driving your washing rituals. If you've been practicing the previous exercises, you've demonstrated that you have courage enough to meet this challenge. Furthermore, the desensitization you have already experienced should make this exercise no more difficult than the ones you've completed. Here are the steps:

1. Exposure will be practiced in three phases. Practice phase one by obtaining information on donating blood from donation centers, the Internet, your doctor, or other sources, and learn how the procedure works. Go over the material as many times as necessary to eliminate any anxiety it causes. The more you learn about it, the more you will desensitize yourself to the actual experience.

    Betty visited the Red Cross's Web site, www.give life.org, and downloaded information on the process and answers to frequently asked questions. This assured her the procedure was safe. Nevertheless, going over the material the first time did cause some apprehension. After reviewing it several times, not only did she have a clear understanding of what to expect, she also had reduced her anticipatory anxiety by over 50 percent.

2. Practice phase two of exposure before donating by visiting a donation location, meeting some of the staff, and letting them know that you haven't donated before and are naturally apprehensive about it. Ask them lots of questions. They'll be pleased for the opportunity to show off their knowledge and be supportive. They may even offer you coffee or orange juice and a donut! Also, try to touch things and shake hands. If you must use avoidance, that's okay for now. You'll have future opportunities to do exposures.

    Betty visited the facility and liked the cordiality and professionalism of the staff. She also observed donors actually giving blood and was impressed by how relaxed they appeared. The visit helped to lower her anxiety another notch, although she consciously avoided touching things.

3. Practice the final stage of exposure by selecting a donation location, making an appointment, keeping it, and donating blood.

   Betty followed through and donated. It took about an hour, and by the time it was over she was relieved and felt she had accomplished something for herself and others.

4. Practice ritual prevention over the course of this process on those occasions when you have OCD-driven urges to wash or use false fear-blockers. Be especially wary of using reassurance and avoidance to block exposures.

   During the three phases of the exposure part of this exercise, Betty felt the need to get reassurance from Juan whenever she had thoughts of HIV, but she suppressed them most of the time. Once in a while she asked Juan for assurance that donating blood was safe. Remembering that reassurance was harmful, he reminded her of that. Although she was sticking to the scheduled number of hand washings per day, she noticed they were getting longer. So, she shortened them.

5. Practice awareness by letting the scary thoughts in, noticing physical distress and urges to wash.

   By now Betty was finding it fairly easy to accept thoughts of contracting HIV and AIDS. She was beginning to become detached from them, even seeing them as ridiculous. The physical sensations that went with the obsessions were mild as were infrequent urges to wash. Now she knew she had the tools for recovery.

6. Continue donating blood until you're no longer anxious about it. By then your OCD should be much improved.

   Betty made additional donations without any misgivings. This boosted her confidence and self-esteem. She had transformed her suffering into a salvation for others.

EXPOSURE EXERCISES IN IMAGINATION

Illness and disease are the imagined consequences of contact with blood and things it contaminates. So, just as you did exposure exercises to tangible triggers, it is necessary to do exposures to imagined triggers by using imaginary means. You can do this by writing about your thoughts and images of dreaded future events. Refer to chapter 5 for a full description of this technique. After you've developed a scenario, practice exposure to it by rewriting and rereading it for periods of time long enough to feel a distinct drop in initial fear aroused by the exercise. You can also record your story on a endless-loop tape and listen to it for prolonged periods of time. You'll notice that your fear will go down on its own without washing being required! Here's an example of a scenario that Betty wrote and recorded about the contents of her obsessions over the time she was doing the blood donation exercise.

■ Betty's Story: An Imagined Scenario

Is this really safe? Should I really do this? I see myself lying on the table with the blood draining from my arm, and I wish I wasn't here. I should have just stayed with the other exposure exercises; this one is just too dangerous. I feel like leaving right now, but it's probably too late. I'll just have to suffer through this. No matter how safe they try to be, there's no guarantee their instruments are not contaminated with the AIDS virus which is now in me. I'll live to regret this, however long that might be. I should have just stayed with the other exercises and been satisfied with the progress I made with them. Now I'm going to worry even more about HIV and AIDS. It takes years before it can be diagnosed and I can't stand to think of passing those years with these thoughts on my mind and these anxious feelings in my body. All I'll be able to think about is if and when I'll start having symptoms. I'll be constantly checking myself for every little thing to make sure it's not the start of the disease. The anxiety will be unending and the possible consequences will be fatal. If only I hadn't taken this step, I wouldn't have these problems. When will this be over, or will it ever be over?

Betty listened to the tape many times before and after donating. Over this period her anxiety decreased from moderate to mild. After the donation, there was a modest increase in her anxiety, and Betty continued using the tape, which eventually brought her anxiety down to almost zero. She continued donating blood, which in turn produced further desensitization to the point where she had only occasional, mild recurrences of her symptoms. When this happened, she practiced ERPA and they abated.

Summary

This chapter focused on exercises to desensitize you to a commonly feared bodily substance—blood. By reducing your fears to it, your fears of other situations associated with blood will also be reduced. Therefore, for the best results it is important that you continue to make contact with situations you have previously avoided, if only for the purpose of consolidating your gains. The last chapter in this book discusses ways you can maintain your improvement.

CHAPTER 8

Hindrances, Helpers, and Holding On to Success

The first part of this chapter covers common obstacles that hinder recovery. The second part covers general guidelines for helping and living with people recovering from OCD. The final section provides recommendations for maintaining and promoting ongoing recovery from OCD.

HINDRANCES

As you know by now, recovery from OCD cannot be achieved without exposure to your obsessional fears. Therefore, most causes of treatment failure are due to improper execution of the exposure exercises. These generally fall under the following categories:

- Insufficient exposure

- Incomplete exposure in reality

- Incomplete exposure in imagination

- Incomplete ritual prevention

- Nonadherence to treatment guidelines

Insufficient Exposure

Insufficient exposure is most often a result of practicing exercise sessions intermittently or ending them before the distress drops. To correct this, practice sessions should be done on a daily basis (including weekends and holidays) for enough time to notice a significant drop in the distress triggered by the exposures. The exposure session should never stop while your SUDS levels are high. Doing so can further sensitize you to fear. To prevent this, you should practice anywhere from forty-five minutes to an hour and a half. If your anxiety doesn't come down after an hour and a half, it means the exposure exercise is too strong and you should substitute an easier one for it.

Insufficient exposure can also result from not practicing a particular exercise enough times. The exercises should continue until your SUDS levels are 0 or close to it. It's even recommended that you continue practicing at this level so feelings of being anxiety free will become associated with a trigger that previously provoked anxiety. This helps ensure that the trigger will remain nonthreatening.

Incomplete Exposure In Reality

Incomplete exposure in reality can be corrected by practicing exposure exercises for all of the items you checked that trigger rituals. This means the most difficult ones as well as the mild and moderate ones. All too often people will accept a partial improvement in their OCD. They choose to live with the weakened symptoms rather than complete the exposure exercises. If you do this, the symptoms will gradually regain their intensity and eventually become full-blown. Practicing exposure to all of the triggers can prevent this type of symptom return.

Incomplete Exposure in Imagination

Incomplete imaginal exposures can be prevented by:

- Exposure to the content of your obsessions. For example, people with an obsession they might contract AIDS if they touch a man that "looks like" he has AIDS need imaginal exposure to thoughts and images of touching men who "look like" they have AIDS.

- Exposure to the feared consequences of the obsession. In the case above, the feared consequence is contracting AIDS.

Incomplete exposure can result from escape hatches included in audiotaped scenarios. You have been given instructions for writing scenarios and recording them to use for exposure exercises (see chapter 5). When people do this, they tend to include escape hatches like reassuring statements. These provide brief relief, but are false fear-blockers. As such they detract from the benefits of the exercise. For example, one woman with obsessions about getting sick from contamination made a tape interspersed with the phrase, "I know these thoughts are my OCD." This phrase, of course, reduced her anxiety and weakened the impact and effectiveness of the tape.

For complete exposure, remember to consider visual exposures, for example, pictures and videotapes with images and scenes that trigger your fears and rituals. Use them just as you would audiotapes. View them repeatedly for extended periods of time for desensitization.

Incomplete Ritual Prevention

Incomplete ritual prevention can result from a failure to stop mental rituals. Many times these go unrecognized because they can be in the form of rational arguments against the irrationality of your fears. More obvious internal or covert rituals come in the form of counting mentally; repeating certain words, phrases, or number sequences; or praying. A common mental ritual for those with the fear they accidentally touched something that was contaminated is to "replay" their movements in imagination to assure themselves they didn't touch the wrong thing. You can identify mental rituals and the intentional use of any mental activity following an obsession because they reduce distress. Once identified, refrain from using them and receive the benefits of desensitization from the resulting exposure.

Nonadherence to Treatment Guidelines

If you don't practice the treatment exercises, obviously you won't get better. Avoidance of treatment can start with just thinking about practicing anxiety-provoking activities on a daily basis, which is usually enough to cause a person to feel nervous. This is called anticipatory anxiety and is procrastination's best friend. Keep in mind that anticipation can be worse than realization. You'll find this true for this work. The benefits you'll feel from the exposure activities will outweigh the distress you anticipate performing it. So get started and practice the exercises regularly. Here are a few things that may help:

- Schedule your exposures on specific days and times set aside exclusively for this purpose.

- Use positive reinforcement by rewarding yourself for adhering to the schedule. For example, after each exercise do or give yourself something nice that you can earn only by doing the exercises.

- Recognize the courage you're demonstrating by going through this difficult treatment.

HELPING AND LIVING WITH A PERSON WITH OCD

Those who are close to people with OCD are frequently in a quandary as to what actions to take in helping them in their recovery. The following guidelines recommend actions you can take (and those you should avoid) that will promote the development of optimal functioning in the person you're concerned about.

Educate Yourself about OCD

Your first step is to learn about the nature and treatment of the disorder. Read chapter 1 of this book and you'll get a general understanding of the symptoms, their causes, and how they're treated with behavior therapy. Although this book focuses on one subtype of OCD that results in washing rituals, in the Resources section I have included a list of books about OCD in general. A major source of information is the OC Foundation. It is an organization dedicated to assisting people with OCD and their family and friends. It supports research into the causes and effective treatments of OCD and related disorders. The membership is made up of people with OCD, their families, professionals, and other interested individuals. The foundation provides a bimonthly newsletter with articles written by people with OCD, mental-health practitioners, and researchers. The organization also provides referrals to practitioners and support groups. Contact information for the organization is also in the Resources section.

It's Not a Matter of Willpower

People with OCD cannot will themselves to stop doing rituals any more than they can stop the intrusive, repetitive, anxiety-provoking thoughts, images, and urges that are one of the defining symptoms of the disorder. Their rituals and obsessions are a result of neural circuits in the brain that have gone awry. Yelling "Stop doing that" at a person achieves, at best, only temporary suppression of rituals which will resurface in your absence. In fact, barking commands can cause rituals to increase from the stress of being pressured by demands the sufferer cannot meet. Keep in mind that their symptoms torment them more than they do you. Ultimately, with the aid of this book, a behavior therapist, or both, the person can learn to eliminate their symptoms.

OCD Is Not a Psychotic Disorder

People with OCD often wonder whether it's a form of craziness. It isn't. They may occasionally doubt their sanity, because what they know conflicts with what they feel. While they know that their obsessive fears are unrealistic, when they are in the grip of these fears they seem real. In addition, they realize that the ritualistic behaviors used to dampen their fears are always excessive and frequently inappropriate. You can help by not doing or saying things that could reinforce doubts about the person's sanity. The OCD symptoms are distressing enough without added misery from a misconception of being psychotic.

How Recovery Is Learned

People with OCD are taught to perform a series of exercises that releases them from their symptoms. The exercises involve gradually exposing the person to the triggers for their obsessive fears. With sufficient exposure, the brain's fear system stops responding to false alarms of danger, because the obsessional fear is always irrational and therefore cannot really happen. Then the rituals stop, because they no longer have a purpose. When the obsessions are occurring, rituals are done to reduce the distress from them. With no obsessions, there's no need for rituals. The exposure exercises are scheduled in a systematic way that starts with exposures to mild or moderate triggers for fear and gradually moves to the most anxiety provoking.

Ask How You Can Help

Let the person know you are willing to help him or her with their symptoms. For example, you could gently encourage them to minimize or refrain from ritualizing, assist them in completing exposure exercises, or provide other support that would help promote recovery. If your offer is refused, accept that. If it's accepted, work out the specifics of your role as a helper and go forward.

Consulting with a Therapist

If the person you're concerned about is receiving treatment from a mental-health professional, ask the person if you can meet with their therapist to get recommendations for being an effective helper. Assure the person that you have no intentions of invading their privacy and will keep confidential any information they don't wish to disclose. When meeting with the therapist, try to get specific suggestions for ways you can support the person's recovery. Some of the exercises in this book include the participation of helpers.

If the person you're concerned about refuses to seek treatment, continue to remind them, every now and then, that their disorder is highly treatable. But be careful not to be overbearing by insisting they get help. This can backfire and cause the person to resist treatment even more. You can provide them with written information in the form of self-help books, the OCD Newsletter, and other sources (see the resources section that follows this chapter). Also, consider consulting with a mental-health professional who has expertise in treating OCD. An experienced therapist may be able to help you motivate the person to make an appointment, help you to manage your feelings of frustration constructively, and make recommendations as to how you can be helpful and not harmful to the person.

Participating in Avoidance Perpetuates Avoidance

You might be moved to help someone who is in a state of exhaustion from ritualizing for hours by granting their request to handle things they're afraid to touch. Don't do it. You are not helping the person but harming them, because you're providing only temporary relief. By helping the person avoid contact with contamination, you're preventing them from having exposure to the very situations they need to face in order to recover. What's more, their symptoms will worsen and their requests for help will increase correspondingly. For example, I worked with a man whose avoidance of objects in his own home was so extreme that his wife had to pour bottled water into his opened mouth because he wouldn't touch their drinking glasses.

Reassurance Is Harmful, Not Helpful

People with OCD frequently ask for reassurance that their obsessional fears won't come true. Despite repeated assurance they won't, they are not reassured. At best, the person with OCD gets only a brief and temporary respite from distress like that from other rituals. As such, it blocks exposure to fear which blocks recovery. You can identify the reassurance request because it always comes in the form of being asked a question that's been asked multiple times. The readers for whom this book is intended have been advised in chapter 4 to refrain from asking for reassurance. If they persist, you can remind them that reassurance is not helpful but instead harmful and therefore you're not going to reply. I have found that many times, stopping reassurance can have the single most profound impact on eradicating OCD symptoms.

However, do answer questions that are not repeatedly asked. For example, people with OCD can lose touch with how much washing is appropriate and may say so. Provide them with the information once, twice at most. Usually there's no difficulty identifying what is a reassurance request and what isn't, because the persistence of the requester can become as burdensome to the reassurer as rituals are to the sufferer.

Not responding to reassurance requests should be limited only to matters concerning OCD. Everyone needs occasional reassurance in the course of daily existence, and people with OCD should receive this benefit as well when it's not for the purpose of avoiding obsessional fear. For more on reassurance rituals, read the section in chapter 4 titled "Reassurance Seeking."

Be Truthful

Don't tell "white lies" to the sufferer even though you think you're doing it in their best interest. This happens when, for example, you tell the person that they won't encounter triggers in a particular situation when you know they will. You may consider this a lesson that is exposing them to the situation to show them they can cope with more than they think. Not only is this a manipulation, it's a threat to your relationship and compromises your trustworthiness as a helper.

Accentuate the Positive

Make positive comments about the small changes you see. Remember to praise the person for practicing the exposure exercises, regardless of their outcomes. If they are practiced daily, benefits will occur. Praise is a powerful motivator for change. It's equally important to eliminate the negative. To be an effective helper is to be warm, supportive, and to use friendly persuasion and never coercion. For example, the person may experience a worsening of some symptoms on certain days; however, this does not mean their overall condition is indeed worsening. If the sufferer complains of this, simply remind him or her that tomorrow is another day to practice the techniques for overcoming the disorder. Instead of paying too much attention to sporadic fluctuations in symptoms, remind them to pay attention to trends in improvement over time. It's quite normal during the course of treatment that there will be bad days. They do not forecast a bad treatment outcome.

Avoid Overprotection

People with OCD have a serious health problem and to some extent are disabled. Nevertheless, they are capable, to some degree, of performing many of the normal activities of daily living. Despite their relative competence, loved ones are often tempted to take over even the simplest responsibilities from the person in an effort to help them. Unfortunately, relieving them of basic duties tends to cause the individual to perceive himself or herself as more disabled than they actually are. This can be an outcome of overprotection and an example of casting the person in the patient role. In this position, the person's mood is liable to worsen, feelings of hopelessness and helplessness to intensify, and their activity level to decrease. You can help prevent this by maintaining expectations of the person that are not affected by their symptoms. This means expecting them to be as self-sufficient as possible and attentive to their responsibilities and obligations to others, within any limits imposed by their disorder.

Pleasant Activities Are a Requirement, Not an Option

Most people with OCD have some degree of depression. This can result in decreased participation in activities that the person previously enjoyed. When others suggest they get out and do something fun, their reply is often, "When I feel better." It doesn't work like that. The person has to start doing things first, then they will feel better. One can't control their emotions directly, but one can control their muscles. This means getting them in motion doing activities they enjoy. Pleasure will follow.

HOLDING ON TO SUCCESS

Several studies have followed up on patients who have been successfully treated for OCD with behavior therapy and found that for six months or more after treatment, the majority of them remain improved, and some even continued to get better with ongoing outpatient treatment. One example of this is from a study my colleagues and I conducted at the UCLA Neuropsychiatric Institute (Bystritsky et al. 1996). In the study, fifty-eight patients with a diagnosis of severe OCD were treated with exposure therapy in a program they attended for six hours per day, Monday through Friday, for about four weeks. Fifty-five percent finished that program with only mild symptoms. Most of them sustained their improvement at six, twelve, and eighteen months after discharge, and many showed further improvement with continued outpatient management. This predicts that you can maintain your improvement after completing this self-help program, and further improvement is possible from your continued self-management.

To maximize your chances of maintaining your success, follow these guidelines:

- At the first sign of any increase or return of OCD symptoms, practice ERPA until you have desensitized yourself to the situation that triggered the resurgence of the symptoms. Also make it a practice to have frequent contact with situations that previously triggered washing and refrain from doing it. If circumstances arise that trigger fairly strong fears, design exposure activities using the model exercises in chapters 5, 6, and 7 to eradicate washing urges.

- During times of stress, you may become susceptible to increased urges to ritualize. If you're under pressure from school, work, family, or other difficult life situations, be on the alert for giving too much attention to activities that previously triggered washing. This is frequently a sign that compulsive washing is just around the corner. Stress can also be triggered by the occurrence of positive events, such as graduating from school, getting a new job, moving, getting married, or having a baby. This means that during stressful times, be on the alert for increasing urges to wash by monitoring yourself for any heretofore unnoticed washing. It's inevitable that you will have times of stress in your life. Learning to manage them will help you control symptom return and enjoy additional health benefits as well. Learning how to relax and enhancing your social skills and problem-solving abilities are useful ways of moderating life's stresses and strains and curbing washing.

■ It's not unusual for people with OCD to have other psychological problems that are stressful and threaten recovery. Depression is one of the most frequent. Usually the depression lifts with improvement in the OCD. However, if you have a persistent low mood following significant improvement in your OCD, consultation with a cognitive behavioral therapist or psychiatrist—who may suggest cognitive behavioral therapy or prescribe medications or both—is recommended. Other anxiety disorders can also coexist with OCD, such as social phobia, panic disorder, and post-traumatic stress disorder. If you continue to be anxious after getting your OCD under control, consider consultation with a mental-health practitioner to identify any other anxiety conditions. If any are diagnosed, get treatment. They are all highly responsive to cognitive behavioral therapy and medications used either in combination or alone.

■ If you spent considerable time engaged in obsessions and performing rituals, your occupational and social functioning may have become significantly impaired.

Once your symptoms are improved, you may have considerable time on your hands. Use it to improve your vocational, educational, and social interests by looking into various employment or educational opportunities, participating in volunteering, and establishing social relationships. You want to focus on the outer world to counteract tendencies of focusing on your inner world and its potential OCD hazards.

KEEP ON KEEPING ON

Do not allow others to do things for you that you can do for yourself or excuse you from responsibilities that you're capable of meeting, nor to restrict you from fulfilling your capabilities and pursuing your interests and activities. Do not regard yourself as essentially different from "normal people," "an obsessive," or "a compulsive." You are not a disorder, but a person with a disorder who, with great courage and determination, faced, embraced, and erased it. You've proven yourself capable of this great achievement, which signifies your potential for many more successes.

Good Luck!

Resources

SELF-HELP BOOKS

Baer, Lee. 2001. *Imp of the Mind: Exploring the Silent Epidemic of Obsessive Bad Thoughts*. New York: Plume.

————. 2002. *Getting Control: Overcoming Your Obsessions and Compulsions*. New York: Plume.

Ciarrocchi, Joseph W. 1995. *The Doubting Disease: Help for Scrupulosity and Religious Compulsions*. Mahwah, NJ: Paulist Press.

Foa, Edna B., and Michael J. Kozak. 1997. *Mastery of Obsessive-Compulsive Disorder: Client Workbook*. San Antonio: The Psychological Corporation, Harcourt Brace & Co.

Foa, Edna B., and Reid Wilson. 2001. *Stop Obsessing: How to Overcome Your Obsessions and Compulsions*. New York: Bantam Books.

Gravitz, Herbert L. 2004. *Obsessive Compulsive Disorder: New Help for the Family*. Santa Barbara, CA: Healing Visions Press.

Greist, John H. 1993. *Obsessive Compulsive Disorder in Children and Adolescents: A Guide.* Madison, WI: Dean Foundation for Health, Research, and Education.

Munford, Paul. 2004. *Overcoming Compulsive Checking.* Oakland, CA: New Harbinger Publications, Inc.

Neziroglu, Fugen, Jerome Bubrick, and Jose A. Yaryura-Tobias. 2004. *Overcomimg Compulsive Hoarding.* Oakland, CA: New Harbinger Publications, Inc.

Neziroglu, Fugen, and Jose A. Yaryura-Tobias. 1995. *Over and Over Again: Understanding Obsessive-Compulsive Disorder.* New York: Lexington Books.

Osborn, Ian. 1998. *Tormenting Thoughts and Secret Rituals: The Hidden Epidemic of Obsessive-Compulsive Disorder.* New York: Pantheon Books.

Steketee, Gail, and Karen White. 1990. *When Once Is Not Enough: Help for Obsessive-Compulsives.* Oakland, CA: New Harbinger Publications, Inc.

BOOKS FOR PROFESSIONALS

Jenke, Michael A., Lee Baer, and William E. Minichiello, eds. 1998. *Obsessive-Compulsive Disorders: Practical Management.* 3rd ed. St. Louis, MO: Mosby, Inc.

March, John S., and Karen Mulle. 1998. *OCD in Children and Adolescents: A Cognitive-Behavioral Treatment Manual.* New York: Guilford Press.

Swinson, Richard P., Martin M. Antony, S. Rachman, and Margaret A. Richter, eds. 1998. *Obsessive-Compulsive Disorder: Theory, Research, and Treatment.* New York: Guilford Press.

Yaryura-Tobias, Jose A., and Fugen Neziroglu. 1997. *Biobehavioral Treatment of Obsessive-Compulsive Spectrum Disorders.* New York: W. W. Norton.

ORGANIZATIONS

Anxiety Disorders Association of America
8730 Georgia Avenue, Suite 600
Silver Spring, MD 20910
(240) 485-1001, Fax (240) 485-1035
Web site: www.adaa.org

Association for Behavioral and Cognitive Therapies
305 Seventh Avenue, 16th floor
New York, NY 10001
(212) 647-1890, Fax (212) 647-1865
Web site: www.aabt.org

Madison Institute of Medicine
7617 Mineral Point Road, Suite 300
Madison, WI 53717
(608) 827-2470, Fax (608) 827-2479
Web site: www.miminc.org

OC Foundation
676 State Street
New Haven, CT 06511
(203) 401-2070, Fax (203) 401-2076
Web site: www.ocfoundation.org
E-mail: info@ocfoundation.org

References

American Psychiatric Association. 1980. *Diagnostic and Statistical Manual of Mental Disorders.* 3rd ed. Washington, DC: American Psychiatric Association.

American Psychiatric Association. 1994. *Diagnostic and Statistical Manual of Mental Disorders.* 4th ed. Washington, DC: American Psychiatric Association.

Antony, M., F. Downie, and R. Swinson. 1998. Diagnostic issues and epidemiology in obsessive-compulsive disorder. In *Obsessive-Compulsive Disorder: Theory, Research, and Treatment,* edited by R. Swinson, M. Antony, S. Rachman, and M. Richter. New York: Guilford Press.

Baxter, L. J., J. M. Schwartz, K. S. Bergman, M. P. Szuba, B. H. Guze, J. C. Mazziotta, A. Alazraki, C. E. Selin, H. K. Ferng, P. Munford, and M. E. Phelps. 1992. Caudate glucose metabolic rate changes with both drug and behavior therapy for obsessive-compulsive disorder. *Archives of General Psychiatry* 49(9):681-689.

Billett, E., M. Richter, and J. Kennedy. 1998. Genetics of obsessive-compulsive disorder. In *Obsessive-Compulsive Disorder: Theory, Research, and Treatment*, edited by R. Swinson, M. Antony, S. Rachman, and M. Richter. New York: Guilford Press.

Bystritsky, A., P. R. Munford, R. M. Rosen, K. M. Martin, T. Vapnik, E. E. Gorbis, and R. C. Wolson. 1996. A preliminary study of partial hospital management of severe obsessive-compulsive disorder. *Psychiatric Services* 47:170-174.

Esman, A. H. 2001. Obsessive-compulsive disorder: Current views. *Psychoanalytic Inquiry* 21(2):145-156.

Foa, E. B., and M. J. Kozak. 1996. Psychological treatment for obsessive-compulsive disorder. In *Long-term Treatments of the Anxiety Disorders*, edited by M. R. Mavissakalian and R. F. Prien. Washington, DC: American Psychiatric Press.

Foa, E. B., G. Steketee, R. M. Turner, and S. C. Fischer. 1980. Effects of imaginal exposure to feared situations in obsessive-compulsive checkers. *Behaviour Research and Therapy* 18:449-455.

Hanna, G. L. 1995. Demographic and clinical features of obsessive-compulsive disorder in children and adolescents. *Journal of the American Academy of Child and Adolescent Psychiatry* 34:19-27.

Ingram, I. M. 1961. Obsessional illness in mental hospital patients. *Journal of Medical Science* 107:382-402.

Jenike, M. A. 1991. Geriatric obsessive-compulsive disorder. *Journal of Geriatric Psychiatry and Neurology* 4:34-39.

Karno, M., J. M. Golding, S. B. Sorenson, and M. A. Burnam. 1988. The epidemiology of obsessive-compulsive disorder in five U.S. communities. *Archives of General Psychiatry* 45(12):1094-1099.

Kolada, L., R. C. Bland, and S. C. Newman. 1994. Obsessive-compulsive disorder. *Acta Psychiatrica Scandinavica* Suppl. 376:24-35.

LeDoux, J. 1996. *The Emotional Brain*. New York: Simon & Schuster.

Merck Manual of Medical Information. 1997. Edited by R. Berkow, M. H. Beers, and A. J. Fletcher. Whitehouse Station, NJ: Merck Research Laboratories.

Meyer, V. 1966. Modification of expectations in cases with obsessional rituals. *Behavior Research and Therapy* 4:273-280.

Muris, P., H. Merckelbach, and M. Clavan. 1997. Abnormal and normal compulsions. *Behaviour Research and Therapy* 35:249-252.

Neziroglu, F., R. Anemone, and J. A. Yaryura-Tobias. 1992. Onset of obsessive-compulsive disorder in pregnancy. *American Journal of Psychiatry* 149:947-950.

Rachman, S., and P. De Silva. 1978. Abnormal and normal obsessions. *Behaviour Research and Therapy* 16:233-248.

Rasmussen, S. A., and M. T. Tsuang. 1986. Clinical characteristics and family history in DSM-III obsessive-compulsive disorder. *American Journal of Psychiatry* 143:317-322.

Rudin, E. 1953. Ein beitrag zur frage zwangskranheit insebesondere inhere hereditarian beziehungen. *Archiv für Psychiatrie und Nervenkrankheiten* 191:14-54.

Swedo, S., H. Leonard, and L. Kiessling. 1994. Speculations on anti-neuronal antibody-mediated neuropsychiatric disorders of childhood. *Pediatrics* 93(2):323-326.

Yaryura-Tobias, J., J. Todaro, M. S. Grunes, D. McKay, R. Stockman, and F. A. Neziroglu. 1996. *Comorbidity versus continuum of Axis I disorders in OCD.* Paper presented at the meeting of the Association for Advancement of Behavior Therapy, New York.

Paul R. Munford, Ph.D., is a clinical psychologist and executive director of the Anxiety Treatment Center of Northern California. He is clinical professor in the Department of Psychiatry of the University of California, Davis, School of Medicine, where he teaches cognitive behavior therapy. He sits on the Scientific Advisory Board of the Obsessive Compulsive Foundation and is a member of the American Psychological Association, Anxiety Disorders Association of America, Association for the Advancement of Behavior Therapy, and California Psychological Association.

Some Other New Harbinger Titles

The Cyclothymia Workbook, Item 383X, $18.95

The Matrix Repatterning Program for Pain Relief, Item 3910, $18.95

Transforming Stress, Item 397X, $10.95

Eating Mindfully, Item 3503, $13.95

Living with RSDS, Item 3554 $16.95

The Ten Hidden Barriers to Weight Loss, Item 3244 $11.95

The Sjogren's Syndrome Survival Guide, Item 3562 $15.95

Stop Feeling Tired, Item 3139 $14.95

Responsible Drinking, Item 2949 $18.95

The Mitral Valve Prolapse/Dysautonomia Survival Guide,
Item 3031 $14.95

Stop Worrying Abour Your Health, Item 285X $14.95

The Vulvodynia Survival Guide, Item 2914 $15.95

The Multifidus Back Pain Solution, Item 2787 $12.95

Move Your Body, Tone Your Mood, Item 2752 $17.95

The Chronic Illness Workbook, Item 2647 $16.95

Coping with Crohn's Disease, Item 2655 $15.95

The Woman's Book of Sleep, Item 2493 $14.95

The Trigger Point Therapy Workbook, Item 2507 $19.95

Fibromyalgia and Chronic Myofascial Pain Syndrome, second edition,
Item 2388 $19.95

Kill the Craving, Item 237X $18.95

Rosacea, Item 2248 $13.95

Thinking Pregnant, Item 2302 $13.95

Call **toll free, 1-800-748-6273,** or log on to our online bookstore at **www.newharbinger.com** to order. Have your Visa or Mastercard number ready. Or send a check for the titles you want to New Harbinger Publications, Inc., 5674 Shattuck Ave., Oakland, CA 94609. Include $4.50 for the first book and 75¢ for each additional book, to cover shipping and handling. (California residents please include appropriate sales tax.) Allow two to five weeks for delivery.

Prices subject to change without notice.